MW01518302

T THE
LAST BULLET

TO THE LAST BULLET

The Inspiring Story of
Braveheart - ASHOK KAMTE

26/11 Mumbai Terror Attack-Cama Hospital Incident Unfolded...

VINITA KAMTE
With Vinita Deshmukh

ameya prakashan

© Vinita Kamte

No part of this book may be reproduced, stored in a retrieval system or transmitted in any form or by any means without the prior written permission of the copyright holder.

Publisher
Ulhas Latkar
Ameya Prakashan
207, Business Guild, Law College Road,
Pune 411 004. Tel.: 91-20-25457571
www.ameyaprakashan.com
E-mail: ameyaprakashan@gmail.com

ISBN 978-93-80514-03-1

Cover Design by Aays Ads

Photo pages layout
Nazim Shariff

Printed at
K. Joshi & Co., Pune 30

Second Edition
26th November 2009

Price: Rs. 300

This book is dedicated to
Heroes known and unknown of 26/11

ABOUT THE AUTHORS

Vinita Kamte is the wife of IPS officer, Late Mr. Ashok Kamte, who was additional commissioner, East Region Mumbai, when he was killed in action in the Mumbai terror attack of November 26, 2008. Vinita has graduated in Bachelor of Socio-Legal subjects (BSL), Bachelor of Laws (LLB) and Masters in Labour Laws and Labour Welfare from Symbiosis University, Pune.

vinitakamte@gmail.com

Vinita Deshmukh is a senior journalist of 22 years standing. Presently, she is the editor of *Intelligent Pune,* a pro-active, public journalism weekly, which she launched in 2006. She was the former Senior Editor of the national daily, *The Indian Express,* Pune. An award winning journalist, she has won the prestigious Chameli Devi Jain award (2008) and The Statesman Award for Rural Reporting twice (in 1998 and 2005).

vinitapune@gmail.com

CONTENTS

FOREWORD ix
KAVITA KARKARE

STRAIGHT FROM THE HEART xii
VINITA KAMTE

PROLOGUE xvi
VINITA DESHMUKH

1. THE ENDLESS NIGHT 1

2. THE LAST POST 21

3. ANGER, PAIN & HURT 24

4. WILL SOMEONE TELL ME THE TRUTH? 27

5. TRUTH UNFOLDS 37

6. MY TRYST WITH RTI 62

7. RIOTS AND BATTLES: MUMBAI POSTING 69

8. SALUTES FROM SOLAPUR: SOLAPUR POSTING 78

9. THE BEGINNINGS: BHANDARA POSTING 101

10. WHEN WE MET 118

11. A CHIP OF THE OLD BLOCK: SATARA POSTING 125

12. UNIFORM: A FAMILY TRADITION 137

13. FAIR AND FEARLESS: SANGLI POSTING 158

14. THE FOREIGN ASSIGNMENT: BOSNIA POSTING 168

15. AVID SPORTSMAN AND FITNESS FREAK 171

16. FAMILY AND FRIENDS 184

17. A PASSION FOR WEAPONS 198

18. LETTER FROM A FRIEND 204

19. A NEW DAY, A NEW DREAM 210

BIO-DATA: ASHOK KAMTE 218

FOREWORD

– KAVITA KARKARE

Being a police officer's wife, I have always believed that it is a crime to suffer injustice. Vinita Kamte, who, with undaunted tenacity and perseverance uncovered the truth behind the death of her brave husband, Ashok Kamte – and how he fell to terrorists' bullets on 26/11 - has lived up to this belief. More admirable is the fact, that, she has shown immense strength in rising above her personal grief to speak for her husband, about all that happened in the final hours, revealing his courageous fight with the terrorists under daunting circumstances till his last breath.

I have always seen my husband's leadership through the years, and was therefore surprised when doubts were raised in this particular incident. Thanks to Vinita, I too became aware of my husband Hemant's team leadership in the Cama Hospital incident, wherein he along with Ashok and Mr. Vijay Salaskar dared to take on the terrorists, without support of reinforcement from the

TO THE LAST BULLET

Mumbai Police, despite repeated requests by him. For several days, I was being fed with misinformation regarding the death of my husband. It was made to appear that my husband walked into the lane, sat inside a vehicle and was shot dead by terrorists. To Vinita and her twin sister Revati goes the credit of exposing one of the most shameful acts of cover-up attempted by the authorities to dismiss the officers' bravery as foolhardiness.

It was her courage that gave me the impetus to raise my voice against the sub-standard bullet-proof jackets provided to the police and which Hemant wore on that fateful night. Would he have been saved if the jacket was of international standards is a question that will haunt me for the rest of my life.

Over the years, I have closely watched Ashok's career, which was inspiring, to say the least. If as a young officer, he daringly took on the Naxalites in the deadly terrain of Bhandara, as Additional Commissioner of police, East Mumbai, he astutely controlled last year's MNS riots. Wherever he was posted, he left a mark. I would like to mention that Martyrs are not made in a day's fight. It takes an entire lifetime of dedication and courage to become one. Ashok was born in a family of policemen with outstanding career records. His education in premier schools and colleges further moulded his character. More importantly, he had the unconditional support of his wife, Vinita, who, with her complete dedication to her husband and home, helped him surge forward to achieve tremendous success in his profession.

The making of the book in itself is a story of a police officer's courage and a wife's undying affection for her husband.

I am privileged to have been given the opportunity to write this Foreword.

■

STRAIGHT FROM THE HEART

– VINITA KAMTE

26th November 2008, the Wednesday that changed the way Mumbai lived, was to change my life too forever.

The unprecedented terror attacks on Mumbai due to their very nature showed the police force in glorious light as well as exposed its shortcomings. The Mumbai Police had never faced an attack of this nature or magnitude. The dearth of highly trained personnel, shortage of sophisticated weapons and ammunition and an untrained force to handle such a situation were only some of the shortcomings which came to light. This was probably why some of the Mumbai Police personnel shied away from facing the situation.

On the other hand, realising that it was an added responsibility, a few senior officers displayed qualities of leadership and showed exemplary courage in tackling the situation.

Hemant Karkare, Ashok Kamte and Vijay Salaskar led

their team from the front realising that the constabulary was ill equipped and ill trained to be sent ahead in such a situation. In spite of being ambushed they managed to injure Kasab on both hands incapacitating him. This averted many casualties as the duo moved towards Chowpatty where ASI Ombale and others showed presence of mind and selfless courage in apprehending an injured Kasab. This bravery and exemplary courage showed by some officers from CST to Chowpatty gave to the country the first fidayeen ever to be caught alive.

My husband, Ashok Kamte, Additional Commissioner, East Region, Mumbai, fell to the bullets of the terrorists in the Cama Hospital episode that night.

As the first anniversary of that black Wednesday neared my urge to unravel the mystery grew stronger; it soon became clear that the only way the entire Cama episode can be demystified, is to put across all the circumstances in detail in the form of a book. I did not want the facts to get distorted and in the process the truth to get suppressed or diluted. This book is my tribute to the departed martyrs.

As his wife, my curiosity to understand the course of events which led to Ashok's death was surprisingly met with a series of stumbling blocks from the Mumbai Police. I was refused even a copy of the Post Mortem Report; leave alone the other facts of the circumstances that led to his death.

In this book we piece together, based on official documents, the shocking story of why the officers would not have fallen to the devil's bullets and even if they had, would have perhaps not lost their lives if help had reached them in time and not after a crucial delay of 40 minutes. It is not my status as a senior police officer's wife but the most formidable weapon of the common man, the Right To Information Act (RTI) which provided me with the crucial details.

Ashok's brilliant career record as an IPS officer, wherein he always led from the front, is an inspiring story to hundreds of young aspirants who dream to don the uniform. He is the recipient of the Ashok Chakra – the highest peacetime gallantry award – conferred posthumously on January 26, 2009. Wherever he served, Ashok touched the lives of people – whether by fighting the Naxals in Vidharbha or by crushing the criminal elements in Solapur. His career is an example of how effective the police force can be, when it works with honesty and courage.

Ashok belongs to a family which has served the Nation, in uniform over four generations. In a short span of time, I have to the best of my ability attempted to compile the details of his life and recount his professional story with the accuracy it deserves.

This book is also my personal way of remembering Ashok to the world – as a daring and upright police officer; a considerate boss; an outstanding sportsman; a compassionate human being; a doting husband and father.

This book has been pieced together by Vinita Deshmukh who elucidated my thoughts and narration lucidly and tirelessly. In my endeavour to get to the truth my twin sister Revati Dere's contribution has been invaluable.

I also take this opportunity to thank all my family members , friends and Ashok's loyal staff who gave me unflinching support.

■

PROLOGUE

– VINITA DESHMUKH

It was over a cup of coffee that I offered to write a book for Vinita, on her husband Ashok Kamte. While she had been contemplating a book for some time, it crystallised on that spur of the moment.

Ever since the Mumbai Terror, I had been tracking Vinita's story of how she was being stonewalled by the authorities while trying to find out the circumstances leading to her husband's death. I got further interested in meeting her when she invoked the Right To Information Act (RTI) to procure call log records of communication between the Police Control Room and her husband on the night of 26/11 during the encounter at the Cama Hospital, where he, along with two other stalwart police officers, Mr. Hemant Karkare and Mr. Vijay Salaskar, were killed in action.

Being the editor of a pro-active local weekly tabloid, Intelligent Pune, which uses the RTI Act prolifically for its stories, I was fascinated by Vinita's dogged perseverance in getting to the truth.

Thus, we met one evening to discuss her tryst with RTI. However, in the course of the conversation, Vinita's admiration and pride for her husband shone through as she also narrated bits and pieces of his illustrious career as a police officer. As a journalist I was aware of Ashok's sparkling tenure as Police Commissioner, Solapur but the kaleidoscope which she presented so instantaneously, provided a deeper, awe-inspiring insight into his professional career.

I immediately sensed that Ashok's life too was indeed a big story, which needed to be told, on a far larger canvas, than merely cramming it into a news item or a soft feature in a newspaper. Besides, she told me how distressed and hurt she sometimes felt about sensational headlines and misleading stories that appeared in the print and electronic media.

Thus began a four month journey of telling the story of an officer and gentleman, which should serve as an inspiration for generations to come.

I travelled to towns where Ashok was posted; spoke to many citizens, his colleagues, friends and family members, to construct a comprehensive story. I listened to Vinita, who poured out her heart, passionately, sometimes with tears streaming down her eyes. I scanned through the maze of newspaper clippings which Vinita has meticulously collected over the 17 years of Ashok's dynamic and action-packed career as a police officer.

In a sense we switched roles. I became the narrator and she the investigative journalist. I decided to pen the story in first person. The book unfolds Ashok's multi-faceted personality as a tough yet humane police officer; of a combat officer with expertise in sophisticated weapons and warfare; an affectionate and loving husband; a doting father; ideal student; affable friend; fitness freak; outstanding sportsman; food and music buff and; much more. It is a story of a man with a 100 per cent commitment to life and work - a rarity, in these days of mediocrity, sycophancy and corruption that has befallen our country.

Just as this book is a salute to a great human being and a stalwart police officer from his wife, it is also the story of grit, determination and unconditional love of a wife whose faith in her husband that he could not have gone down without fighting to the last breath, spurred her to research on his death and compile for posterity, the greatness of his life.

I thank Huned Contractor for editing the book. I thank Mr. Ulhas Latkar of Ameya Prakashan for bringing out the book within the daunting deadline. I also thank my husband, Vishwas for being a pillar of support in this endeavour.

CHAPTER 1

THE ENDLESS NIGHT

26th November, 2008. A Wednesday. The day began like any other for me but would end like no other. The pleasant Pune morning weather belied the misfortune that awaited me. Ashok had come home on the weekend that went by and the house had come alive with laughter and activity as it always did.

Ever since he had been posted as Additional Commissioner, East Region, Mumbai four months ago and was based in Chembur, this was only the second time that he had managed to visit us in Pune. But since our weekends would be so incomplete without him, I, along with our children Rahul, 14 years and Arjun, 8, would drive down to Mumbai every Friday evening and return on Monday. Sometimes Rahul stayed behind in Pune if he had weekend classes and Arjun often missed his school on Monday since we would return only by the evening. I felt a bit guilty about that.

For the first time, in our 17 years of marriage, I sensed

Ashok's feeling of loneliness. This was slightly compensated by the company of Hazel and Hillary, his favourite Basset hounds, who followed their master wherever he went. In his earlier posting at Solapur as the Police Commissioner, he had a doting staff and an amazing cook and had also made a lot of friends. So, even though he had stayed there as a forced bachelor, he had felt quite at home. Mumbai was a different story. He disliked what the cook dished out and being a die-hard foodie, that bothered him a lot. He could have visited his father often, to relish home meals, at his house on Napean Sea Road but Ashok was too conscientious to leave his jurisdiction. Although he was entitled to a better residential accommodation in South Mumbai, he preferred a rented place at the Tata Power Housing Colony in Chembur so that the reaction time would be quicker in case of an emergency.

Understandably then, he would eagerly wait for the weekend so that he could be with us. "Veenz, I trust only you on the expressway with Rahul and Arjun," he would often say. Like about everything, he was proud of my driving skills too. And each time we started off for Mumbai, he would call at least four to five times during the journey and, in typical police fashion, ask, "Location?" He just couldn't wait for us to reach there.

On the particular Friday that just went by, he had decided to come to Pune. "You have been driving up and down too often. Let me come to Pune instead," he had said. He was also concerned about the fact that I had, a few days ago, driven to Satara for a wedding and that it would be a strain to take to the highway once again. Ashok had already forwarded a set of demands before his arrival. "Hope you are making fish fillets?" he had asked me. He had called up my mom and said, "I am coming for lunch on Sunday to have your prawn curry." Rahul and Arjun, but obviously, were as excited as their 'Dadda'.

When we visited my mom, he pointed at the corner table that adorns her living room and told her for the umpteenth time: "Mummy, leave this behind for me." The round wooden table has exquisitely carved elephant heads on each of the four legs. Mom's reply was the same as always: "Take it right now, it is all yours." They were like the best of friends. Before he left for Mumbai on Sunday afternoon, he said to me, "I don't think I can come to Pune before December now. Start doing up the garden for the New Year's Eve party." We always looked forward to this annual bash we hosted – it was that time of the year when we could catch up with our friends and dance and be merry till the wee hours of the morning. Since December 31 was only five weeks away, my mind was already in a whirl about how best to spruce up the garden.

Even when Ashok was not in Pune, there was a predictable routine we followed. I would drop Arjun to his school at 7.45 am and when I returned home at 8 am, Ashok would call me up while sipping his first cup of tea. The phone rang this morning too. Just as usual. "I will be busy with the SPG (Special Protection Group) officers from Delhi. There is a Prime Minister's rally on the Chembur grounds sometime this week and they have come down to check on security arrangements," Ashok said. He had organised lunch for them too. "Later, I am taking Mr. Aranha out for dinner," he added.

Mr. Francis Aranha was his immediate boss as Superintendent of Police, Bhandara when Ashok had been appointed there as ASP (Assistant Superintendent of Police) in 1992. Those who are familiar with the Police and the Indian Police Service would know that for an ASP the relationship with his SP transcends the official and becomes something more. I was newly married then and in that Naxalite-infested and backward region it was the Aranhas who gave us good company and me a lot of moral support. Over the years, we had become close friends. Since he had come down to Mumbai for some court work, he had, as expected, stayed over with Ashok. "It's going to be a long day," Ashok trailed off before hanging up.

My father-in-law wanted to take the family out for dinner that evening. So we went out to the Polka Dots Restaurant at Aundh, close to our home. We decided to have an early dinner as it was school the next day. The aroma of Thai Curry and Steamed Rice lingered on as I drove back home. We were about half-way through when Ashok called up. It was about 9.45 pm. I steered the car to the side to take his call. "Are you watching the television?" he asked. "No, we will be home in ten minutes," I said. "Switch it on as soon as you get home. Some kind of gang war seems to have gripped Mumbai," he stated. His voice had a peculiar tone of nonchalance but I could detect a sense of urgency too. Looking at the puzzled expression on everyone's face, I casually said, "It's nothing. Ashok wants us to see something on the TV."

My mind, however, went into a spin. Ashok wouldn't have called unless there was a reason. I stepped on the accelerator with a sense of anxiety creeping into my mind which was getting stronger by the minute. The fear of something untoward happening to him had been haunting me from the time I had become his bride – the first posting being Bhandara, 17 years back. When we got transferred from there after two years, my heart had jumped in delight – the heaviness of that fear had receded and I had hoped never to feel it again. His was a policing job and the risks didn't have to be spelt out.

The fear kept gathering momentum even as we neared the house. There was a strong reason for it: Ashok had always led from the front—whether it was controlling riots, arresting a politician or shooting down a criminal. Even as I got acclimatised to the role of an IPS officer's wife, I had come to realise that Ashok possessed some exceptional qualities. Besides being adroit at handling sophisticated weapons, he was also one of the rare ones to physically lead his team, no matter what danger lay ahead. I was of course proud of him for such valour and selflessness and wasn't surprised to find him idol-worshipped in Solapur for having restored sanity into its corrupt and criminal social fabric.

I was worried. I kept chanting the *Gayatri Mantra* in my mind and drove faster to reach home. As soon as we were there, I jumped out of the car and rushed to switch on the television. Confusing images and reports of firing in some pockets of South Mumbai assaulted us. I called up my mother and my sisters, Vandana and Revati. They had already been watching the news coverage.

"Mamma, Dadda looks after East Mumbai, doesn't he? This is going on in South Mumbai," Rahul pointed out. Rahul, who was sensitive to my feelings, could read my fear. "That's true, but you know how Dadda is. Being the kind of officer, he could be called to handle any situation in any part of the city," I told Rahul, and reminded him of how he had been put in charge of controlling the MNS riots that had recently taken place in West Mumbai. Rahul wondered why it should be so. There wasn't an answer for that one. Just then I began receiving a stream of phone calls. Ashok's nephew Kushan called up to say that his mother was stranded in the Frangipani Restaurant of Hotel Trident as there was firing inside the hotel.

Another call came from Ashok's cousin Ansul, who was dining at Indigo located just a stone's throw away from Taj Hotel. He said he could hear the sound of AK-47 fire in the vicinity and that a lady with bullet injuries had walked up to the restaurant. He also mentioned that he had called up Ashok who told him that it seemed to be some kind of a gang war. Ashok had advised him to stay put in the restaurant and ask the manager to switch off the lights. I told both of them not to get too tense. I believed that everything would get all right within a few minutes. In fact, I found myself playing Agony Aunt to a number of friends who kept calling me to get the latest news and whose voices seemed to be gripped with fear. The truth was that I had no inkling of what was going on and was just as confused.

Arjun, who had been glued to the TV, suddenly shouted: "Mamma, see Karkare Uncle." Images of Mr. Hemant Karkare, the senior IPS officer and head of the Anti-Terrorist Squad (ATS) donning the bullet-proof jacket outside the CST Station were being flashed. We had met him just a month ago at the Diwali party in Mumbai organised by the police and he had chatted with the kids. Way back in 1992, when Ashok was ASP in Bhandara, Mr. Karkare was Superintendent of Police in the neighbouring Chandrapur District, which was also affected by the Naxal menace. We had known the Karkares ever since. I began to get concerned about Ashok's whereabouts as the initial perception of gang war had been replaced by a confirmed terror attack. I called up Ashok – it was 10.43 pm by my watch. "Where are you at this moment?" I asked. "Mr. Hasan Gafoor (Police Commissioner, Mumbai) has asked me to head towards South Mumbai. I have just started and was, in fact, going to call you," Ashok replied.

At 11.15 pm I called him again. "I am still on the road," he said. "But where exactly are you heading?" I asked. "I am on my way to Hotel Trident," he said. I could feel the urgency in his deep voice.

Arjun was crestfallen. He looked at me, his eyes lined with tears, and said, "Mamma, please call up Dadda immediately and ask him to wear his bullet-proof jacket."

In order to put him at ease, I dialled Ashok's cell number to convey his request. That was at 11.27 pm. "I am on the spot and in the middle of an operation, so don't call me," Ashok told me in a no-nonsensical manner. "Where is Dadda exactly?" Arjun asked. I told him of what I knew. Satisfied with the answer, Arjun went off to sleep. Rahul and I sat glued to the television.

All along I just hoped and prayed that he would be wearing his bullet-proof jacket. I impulsively reached out for the cell phone but controlled the urge to call him again. "He won't like it, and it is not right to call in the middle of an operation," I said to myself.

At around 1.30 am, my friend Netra called up from Mumbai, her voice sounding anguished. "Where is Ashok?" she asked. "I think he is in Hotel Trident," I replied, feeling that familiar sense of anxiety welling up inside me all over again. I had missed watching the television for a few minutes as I was answering calls. "Are you sure he is in Trident?" Netra asked. I couldn't bring myself to reply. I was scared. Thoughts kept rushing into my mind. "Just get back to the news channels. Something seems to have happened," Netra said before hanging up. I rushed to see the news. My feet and hands were now cold with fear. In that micro-second my world stopped. And then it just shattered before me when I saw three words on the television screen – 'Ashok Kamte Shahid.'

Even as the news anchor announced to the world the tragic event, I felt the blood rushing to my head. I went numb. I couldn't believe what I saw and heard. I didn't want to believe it. I was hoping against hope that there was some kind of a mistake. I kept switching the channels for some hope. The story was the same everywhere.

Even as I tried hard to distance myself from the truth, the names of Hemant Karkare and Vijay Salaskar being announced as martyrs could not be ignored. It was true then. It was all happening for real. Rahul, who joined me, was as shell-shocked as I was. "How could this happen to Dadda?" he screamed. I put my arms around his shoulder and held him tight. "Keep quiet, Rahul, or else Arjun will wake up. I am sure there is some mistake," I told him. "But why did Gafoor Uncle send Dadda? Why does he always have to send Dadda?" Rahul screamed, his voice breaking and tears rolling down his face.

I went blank. Somehow, I felt, that I had to take charge.

I heard the clanking of the main gate and the dogs began to bark. Neighbours streamed in. My sister Vandana came along with her husband Hemant, and my mother. My eyes wore a blank, dry look. Arjun being extremely sensitive I did not want to give him this shocking news suddenly. I had to be careful in breaking the news to my father-in-law as he had suffered a stroke recently.

I called up our family doctor and asked her to rush home and keep an ambulance ready for him as a stand-by. I could not take any chances. How would I break the news to Ashok's mother in Delhi who lives alone and to his sister Sharmila in Dubai, I asked myself? But there was no time for any pondering.

I called up one of Ashok's orderlies to ask if he knew in which hospital he was admitted . He gave me the number of a constable who was with Ashok at that point of time. I entered the number in my cell phone but couldn't bring myself to dial it. I wanted my cell phone to ring with Ashok's name on the panel.

But the truth had to be faced. We immediately decided to head for Mumbai. I sat inside the car, not in the driver's seat this time. I instructed everyone at home not to say anything to Arjun. "Only I will break the news after I get back," I said. Vandana and Hemant accompanied me. We were soon on the expressway, heading towards Chembur. It was my turn to call up Ashok and ask: "Location?" But at that moment I didn't want to know that too.

At the Chembur residence, Mr. Aranha, was lying on the sofa watching the television. His tired mind was wavering between sleep and wakefulness. At 1.45 am, he was rudely woken up. The orderly gaspingly said to him, *"Aaple saheb gele* (our boss has gone)." Not having realised the gravity of the statement, Mr. Aranha replied, "Yes, of course I know he has gone. He went in front of me."

The orderly was confused for a moment. With a tremble in his voice, he explained, "No Sir, he has gone forever. He is no more." Mr. Aranha was shocked. Benumbed, he watched the news unfold.

As I was approaching Mumbai, I called up Mr. Aranha. "We are coming there in an hour's time," I informed him. He said he would be waiting and added that he was making enquiries to know what exactly had transpired.

We reached our Chembur residence at around 4.30 am and decided to wait till day break before moving to the Bombay Hospital. This is because the roads were deserted and news of even police vehicles being hijacked by terrorists was making rounds. We were trying to figure out how best to reach the hospital.

From the moment the news of the tragedy struck me, till now I had held myself; controlled my emotions. But now, tears, finally welling up, I sought the refuge of his bedroom. The sight of his clothes which he had just discarded a few hours ago opened the gates. Everything seemed so unreal.

I wanted to know all that had happened between Ashok and Mr. Aranha during the time they had spent with each other before and after dinner. I listened to Mr. Aranha intently. That conversation brought back to my mind a perfectly alive and effervescent Ashok.

At around 6 pm Ashok had come back to his Chembur home, and so did Mr. Aranha. Even after a hard day's work, Ashok never missed his date with the gym and so Mr. Aranha had to patiently wait for him to finish his regular workout. At around 7.45 pm, it was time to go out for the scheduled dinner.

As they set out, Ashok stepped back to check out how

his orderly had prepared his uniform for the next day. Some more time went into the nitty-gritty of the uniform and the orderly was duly advised. "You should have taken the new uniform. I have important meetings to attend tomorrow," Ashok told him. Mr. Aranha could not help being amused. "You are as enthusiastic as you were as an ASP about your uniform," he remarked.

"Why do you carry your AK-47 all the time with you?" Mr. Aranha asked Ashok as they got into the vehicle. "Sir, this is Mumbai and you never know what will happen when," was Ashok's matter-of-fact reply.

Therefore, with the AK-47 propped reassuringly between the front seats, both settled down in the car. It was then that Mr. Aranha noticed the helmet (which Ashok had got when he served for the United Nations in Bosnia) that occupied some of the space. He couldn't help thinking then that Ashok was a police officer too well prepared for any eventuality – his enthusiasm and preparedness had not waned since his ASP days. Mr. Aranha felt proud – after all Ashok was his ASP.

While Ashok was instructing the driver about the place they were to go to, Mr. Aranha stole a quick glance at his friend. "He is so fair and looks so fit that anyone would mistake him for a Westerner," he thought. That apart, his personality was further magnified due to the excellent choice of clothes he wore. At that moment he was wearing a brand new checked shirt that suited him well. "It's a gift from my mother-in-law," Ashok said when he saw Mr. Aranha appreciating his shirt. "She has an excellent taste for clothes," he added. Aranha smiled. He silently admired the way Ashok wore the armour of a tough police officer so invincibly and yet let his childlike exuberance flourish abundantly within him.

They were heading towards the Chembur Golf Course Club and Ashok indicated a short-cut to the driver who, however, did not hear him properly and they were now stuck at a dead-end. Ashok turned to Mr. Aranha and said with a shrug, "He is supposed to follow my instructions when driving but obviously he thinks he knows better. Anyway, the good part is that it will be a longer route now and you will get to see a little more of Mumbai." That was so quintessentially Ashok. He had the ability to take everything in his stride and focus more on the positive spin-off rather than mull over what had gone wrong. It was a trait that had endeared him to many of his colleagues and friends over the years.

"I am thoroughly enjoying this new assignment," Ashok told Mr. Aranha as they drove along and continued, "I have left my family back in Pune but thanks to the expressway the distance does not seem so far. Vinita often drives down here with the kids, but this time around I am going to surprise Rahul on his birthday which is on December 3." Aranha wasn't too convinced. "Are you sure you will get leave?" he asked, knowing only too well the pressures that came with the job of being a senior police officer in a bustling metro like Mumbai. "Yes, I think I would be able to. I mean, I hope so at least. That's why I have not yet told Vinita or the kids anything just in case there is any last minute cancellation. This will be a real surprise and I am quite excited about it," Ashok said.

Unsure of what exactly had prompted him to ask such a question at that point of time, Mr. Aranha had wanted to know if Ashok believed in god. "No, not really. I only believe in *'shastra puja'* (weapon worship)," Ashok had replied with a laugh. They headed towards Chembur Golf Course Club for dinner. As old as 1927 and formally known as The Bombay Presidency Golf Club (BPGC), it remains one of the hottest spots for golfing tournaments. An avid sportsperson, Ashok held sports records in various athletic events and games at school, college and police competitions. Therefore Mr. Aranha wasn't too surprised about this added indulgence. As he took Mr. Aranha around the club, Ashok proudly said, "My father has been prodding me to take to golf for a long time." Ashok's father and his grandfather, Mr. N. M. Kamte, the first Indian IG (equivalent of DG of today) were keen golfers with single digit handicaps. His grandfather in fact, was the Captain of the Poona Golf Club at one time.

"It is night time now and I cannot show you the golf course but let's go to the multi-cuisine restaurant on the first floor which overlooks the Golf Course," Ashok said, guiding Mr. Aranha to the steps. Heads turned as both climbed upstairs, but Ashok was used to such attention, which he let pass. Both decided to have a light dinner, settling for fish and pasta.

"Do you know," Mr. Aranha remarked, "that the only citation I had ever given for recommending a gallantry medal was for you?" Ashok answered with a smile: "Yes,

I have preserved that citation in my file."

Just as they were finishing dinner, Ashok's cell phone rang. It was a call from Ansul. His voice was full of anxiety as he had heard gun shots.

Ashok instantly called up the Police Control Room to find out what was happening. "Two people have opened fire at one another, Sir," was the reply. He called back Ansul and said there seemed to be some sort of a gang war going on and it would be best if he did not stir out of the restaurant.

Half an hour later, Ansul heard the sound of gunshots from the direction of the Taj Hotel. He called up Ashok again, impatient to not only inform him about what was going on but also to find out more about this escalating and fearful situation of violence. Ashok was now worried but the true professional that he was, his voice remained stable when he told Ansul not to worry. "The police will soon have it under control. Just don't step outside till everything is normal," he told his cousin. That was the last that Ansul ever heard from Ashok. Between 10.30 and 11 pm, Ansul desperately tried to call up Ashok, but there was no reply.

Ashok and Mr. Aranha by then had already stepped out of the Chembur Golf Course Club. Ansul's calls had turned a casual evening into something serious. Anxiety gnawed Ashok's mind as he wondered if the situation unfolding in that part of South Mumbai was something more than just a gang war. Not wishing to take any chances, Ashok decided that he would put his jurisdiction on red alert so as to be prepared for any eventuality. "Let us go back home so that I can be ready for any contingency and be easily available should something drastic take place," he told Mr. Aranha. This time when Mr. Aranha once again saw the AK-47 and the helmet in the car, they did not look odd or out of place any more. It was true what Ashok had said earlier: "This is Mumbai and anything can happen any time."

As they drove back home, Ashok's thoughts were fully focused on all the things he must do to keep the East Region of Mumbai under tight control. Calling up one of his officers, he said: "Implement *nakabandi* (checking of all vehicles at important junctions) immediately. Keep all weapons ready and wait for further instructions from me." The moment they reached home, the first thing Ashok did was to switch on the television. The news channels had already started beaming live coverage and were desperately trying to gather bits and pieces of a seemingly 'war-like situation'.

Ashok then called out to his constable Jaywant Patil and asked him to load the boot of the car with stun gas grenades, tear gas shells and ammunition. This was done as a matter of routine whenever he anticipated action of any kind. He asked his staff to stay back instead of returning to their respective homes and instructed his cook to make omelettes for them.

Mr. Aranha who had been watching the news pointed out, "Look there has been an incident of firing at the Chhatrapati Shivaji Terminus." Both watched the images of Mr. Karkare donning a bullet-proof jacket outside CST. The names of police officers who had reached various spots were constantly being flashed.

A few minutes later Ashok's phone rang. It was a call from Mr. Hasan Gafoor, Police Commissioner, Mumbai. It was a short conversation during which Ashok moved out of the living room on to the verandah. Coming back to where Mr. Aranha was seated, he said, "Mr. Gafoor has asked me to come out on the road." Mr. Aranha was nonplussed. "Road? But why? Everything is quiet in your area," he said. Ashok replied, "He wants me to head towards South Mumbai."

There was no time to be wasted. He asked his driver to head towards South Mumbai via the Bombay Port Trust Road since it would be a shorter route.

At around 5.30 am, as we finally set out to go to Bombay Hospital, we were told that Ashok was being shifted to the J. J. Hospital. Revati, my twin sister who lives in Mumbai, and our friends accompanied us to the J. J. Hospital.

I nervously stepped out of the car and entered the ambulance which had arrived carrying Ashok . I saw him lying there peacefully. I touched his cheeks. They had turned cold. I stood there motionlessly as I heard the doctor rattle off the causes of Ashok's death. He had received bullet injuries on his shoulder and head, the doctor said. "But wasn't he wearing a helmet?" I managed to ask. They showed us his blue helmet, which had two holes in it.

At the hospital, they also told me that his gunman,

Constable Jaywant Patil, who had shadowed him through thick and thin, had also been killed. Patil, I knew had two children. A strong sense of shared grief overwhelmed me and my heart went out to the family. I asked the orderlies if the news of his death had been conveyed to his family. It had not been done. I requested the orderlies and Ashok's staff to make sure that they were attended to and to take care of them.

My thoughts once again raced to Ashok's mother, who lived alone in Delhi and sister Sharmila in Dubai. How would I break the news to them? Vandana told me that the servant had woken up my mother-in-law after the news had been flashed on all the television channels. Similarly, Sharmila too had been informed by her friends. She was taking the next flight to Delhi to get her mother along with her to Pune. Ashok's mother adored him. He was the centre of her existence. I wondered whether she would be able to come to Pune, as she had a fall a few months back, which had confined her to her home. I managed to speak to her. She too was clearly devastated. I asked when she would arrive in Pune. She said she would not be able to bear to see her baby, bullet-ridden. "I would like to remember him the way he was – as if he would ring the bell and yell loudly 'Hi Mom' and hug me tightly and suddenly bring life and joy into my being. Let it be that way," she said.

We waited. There were formalities. The post-mortem had to be done. The blank hours went by. At about 8 am we left for Ashok's East Region Office at Chembur. The officers and men wanted a last glimpse of Ashok to pay respects. Then we started for Pune.

The long minutes ticked by. I sat next to Ashok. Soon I realised that there were too many people in the ambulance. I sat solemnly and betrayed nothing of what I was going through. I wanted to hug Ashok and cry on his shoulders before I would once again be surrounded by people after reaching Pune.

The ambulance had travelled hardly for about 15 minutes when it came to a halt. I looked out of the window – there were people and policemen all around. Some were carrying flowers and garlands. "They want to pay homage to Kamte Sir," a policeman in the ambulance informed me. The door opened and people rushed to pay their last respects. Every ten minutes we would be stopped on the road for the same reason.

The halts were endless. The crowds would not stop. I was getting restless. I wanted to reach home quickly and be with Arjun. I also wanted to have some silent moments with Ashok. Finally, when we reached Navi Mumbai I said to Constable Jarag that I would like to be alone with Ashok and that they should shift to another vehicle. I only let my cousin, Manisha, be with me. Those were emotionally shattering moments. I bent down and hugged Ashok. I had so much to say to him. Tears rolled down. I kept hugging him.

My fear was about how to break the news to Arjun. The thought just bled my heart. We were five minutes away from home when Arjun called up "Mamma, what's happened to Dadda? Tell me the truth. Why are there so many people at home? The fear and anxiety in his voice was unnerving. But I tried to keep my voice as calm as I could. "Dadda has got injured. I am coming in five minutes and then I will tell you everything," I said. As soon as I stepped inside the house, I ran upstairs and hugged Arjun. "Dadda got injured trying to save other peoples' lives," I told him. Arjun became breathless and his body began to shiver. He kept shouting at me, "You lied, you lied to me."

Arjun ran downstairs. The living and dining room were packed with people but there was pin-drop silence. "Why are Dadda's eyes shut, Mamma?" asked Arjun in distress and then, "Why is he so cold?" The child's innocent reaction evoked a cry of anguish and sorrow from those present in the room. Arjun asked "Why is everyone laughing at me?" "They are not," I replied. Tears rolled down from many an eye.

We were waiting for Sharmila to reach Pune. She came at around 4 pm and inconsolably broke down. Ashok was not only a brother but a father figure to her—she just couldn't believe that he was gone. The three of us shared a very close bond.

At about 5 pm, the police officers present, gently indicated that the time had come. The final journey was about to begin.

CHAPTER 2

THE LAST POST

Draped in the national flag and bedecked with rose petals and wreaths, Ashok was all set for his last journey. The police cap sat proudly on his chest, the closest thing to his heart.

When he was posted in Solapur as the Police Commissioner, he used to be wary of the treacherous two-lane national highway on which he had to commute often between Solapur and Pune. At times, the driver was reckless. Never the one to be ruffled, he would remark in jest, "I would like to die in action, surely not in an accident."

The cortege began its seven kilometer long journey from home to the Vaikunth Crematorium. My father-in-law, heart-broken, led from the front and it seemed like a sea of humanity surging forward. People from all walks of life were present – more than 10,000. Rahul was

completely distressed but stoically lit the pyre. The army
man's instinct in my father-in-law, who otherwise stood
shattered, manifested at the sounding of the Last Post.
He quickly put up his hand and saluted his brave son
who had sacrificed his life for the nation. Chants of
'Shahid Ashok Kamte Amar Rahe' rent the air. We were all
dazed and went through the funeral proceedings, benumbed. As we started back for home, the feeling of a
deep void stung my heart.

For the next 13 days, the house was teeming with my
near and dear ones who stood by me solidly. I was also
touched by the way people, known and unknown, stood
by me. However, I was not able to find a moment for
myself to reflect on what had happened. One question
that constantly kept haunting me was, "What exactly
happened in those fateful last few hours of that night of
26/11?"

While there seemed to be more details of the incidents
at the Taj, the Trident, the CST and the Nariman House,
somehow the Cama Hospital episode in which the three
dynamic police officers, Mr. Hemant Karkare, Mr. Vijay
Salaskar and Ashok had been killed in action, seemed to
be bereft of information. I could not get a clear picture
either from the official sources or through the print and
electronic media. Like any person would, I was keen on
knowing what exactly transpired that led to the death of
my husband. Being an integral part of the police
fraternity, I was sure the details of those last hours would

be disclosed to me, without any hesitation by the authorities. However this was not to be. I had to go through a trying ordeal to get the facts—even to the extent of taking recourse to the Right to Information (RTI) Act. I soon realised that I was naïve to believe that the system always has a special regard for its heroes.

After a fortnight I realised that I had to come to terms with the new role destiny had forced on me. My near and dear ones had been a great support to me, but eventually I had to mould my life to overcome the loss and grief. And so, I forced everyone to resume their normal routine. Suddenly, the emptiness of the house engulfed us. For the first time, Rahul, Arjun and I together wept openly, pouring out our anguish and grief.

Thereafter, it has been a journey in search of the truth.

■

CHAPTER 3

ANGER, PAIN & HURT

I set out in search of the truth after I let Rahul and Arjun settle a bit at home. I sent them to school from the fourth day itself after Ashok had passed away. I also ensured that Rahul's birthday on December 3 did not pass off uneventfully. Ashok had planned a surprise visit to Pune for Rahul's birthday which was not to be. In an attempt to brighten up the atmosphere, we bought a cake. It was touching to see Rahul offer the first piece of cake to Ashok's photograph.

In the deep recesses of my heart, I bled in pain for having lost Ashok forever but my mind was in deeper anguish. Political bigwigs who visited our home for condolences flung unpalatable statements like "They (meaning Ashok, Mr. Karkare and Mr. Salaskar) did not understand the gravity of the situation." To the nation, the three had instantly become national heroes. Chowks and roadsides of cities, towns and villages in Maharashtra were adorned with hoardings, paying glowing tributes to them.

However, the picture portrayed by the Mumbai Police to the media was that all these three officers got into a vehicle and were instantly shot dead. It was hard for me to fathom that Mr. Karkare who was known for his meticulousness and vision, Mr. Salaskar who was an encounter specialist and Ashok who was always good at quick planning with an undoubted expertise with weapons, would succumb without a fight and a planned strategy.

When Home Minister Mr. R. R. Patil and Director General of Police, Mr. A. N. Roy came home to pay condolences, I gave vent to the anger that was building up within me. I said, "There are police officers who, due to political affiliations, have not been posted out of Mumbai for 10-20 years. They carry on there with impunity. My husband did not believe in sycophancy and accepted with grace any posting or any situation that you put him through. He didn't complain when, during these four months as Additional Commissioner, East Region, you sent him to other regions to handle sensitive situations and despite that, stole away credit from him." (The recent example was the MNS riots for which Ashok was asked to handle although it was in the West Region which was not his jurisdiction. He had efficiently controlled the riots by his astute planning but the information disseminated to the media was that it was the Rapid Action Force which had gloriously handled the situation).

I continued, "While officers of the South Region who shied away from the scene are not being questioned, why are these brave officers who cannot speak for themselves being portrayed as those 'who did not comprehend the situation'?" Both of them quietly heard me out, without comment.

All my grievances against the unfairness of it all poured out within those few minutes. I was deeply hurt, angry and frustrated that those who Ashok had respected in life had failed him in death.

It was then that I decided that I should try and find out the truth. For the sake of the heroes who laid down their lives and for the sake of the sanctity of their sacrifice.

CHAPTER 4

WILL SOMEONE TELL ME THE TRUTH?

Ashok was the Additional Commissioner of Police of the East Region of the Mumbai Police. For those who are familiar with Mumbai, this would mean that he was in charge of the areas around Chembur, Mulund, Ghatkopar, etc. South Mumbai comprises areas like Marine Drive, Colaba, Malabar Hill, Pedder Road, etc. That is the South Region in Mumbai Police parlance. In between lie areas like Dadar, Sion, Matunga, Worli, etc. which is the Central Region. There are two other regions – the West and the North and each of these regions are headed by an Additional Commissioner of Police.

I was not at all surprised that Ashok had been called away from his jurisdiction to douse the fire in a different area. He had been called outside his area on earlier occasions too when some strong action was needed. That was the reputation he had gathered over a number of years; after a number of incidents.

It was pretty clear that the Commissioner of Police

had called him to South Mumbai, when the terrorist firing had started. Ashok had himself told me this on phone at 10.45 pm while on his way to South Mumbai. In fact he had told me that he was headed towards the Trident Hotel.

Then, how and why did he end up, where he ended up?

What happened at the Cama Hospital? Who fired?

How did he die? Was it instantaneous, as people said or was it otherwise?

Why were such confusing and contrasting versions coming out from the investigating agency, in this case the Mumbai Police Crime Branch?

For the first time after the November carnage, I stepped out of Pune on December 24. I had decided to visit the spot the next day where my husband had laid down his life. I was filled with a sense of foreboding. I had not slept for several nights but this night was filled with an uncertain fear and apprehension. I wanted to go, for which I had to muster up all my courage. My sister Revati, my cousin Manisha and her husband Kiran accompanied me when I visited the Rang Bhavan Lane, where Ashok and the others had laid down their lives.

The spot was entirely unlike what I had imagined it to be. It was more like a narrow alley. Hardly the kind of setting one would have thought of for a terrorist ambush and a fire fight.

At the exact spot, photographs of the three heroes, Ashok, Karkare and Salaskar were kept. Agarbattis were lit and flowers offered. A number of people were still coming to place flowers and pay homage. Next to it was an ATM with its shutters down like it had been on that fateful night. The thick metal shutter was riddled with holes. Similar bullets must have hit my husband, I thought. Was he in pain, bleeding, or was it instant? These questions began haunting me. I was physically there but my mind was reliving the fateful incident trying to piece the story together, to understand what exactly happened in those few minutes that had changed my children's and my life forever.

After this we went to the other end of the lane where the Special Branch office is located; then on to the rear gate of the Cama Hospital. These were the areas from where Ashok, Mr. Karkare, Mr. Salaskar and others confronted the situation from the rear of the Cama Hospital before they tried to move to the front of the hospital to take on the terrorists. On way they were ambushed. The details were not clear. Not yet.

A short description of the topography of the area will be useful. Cama Hospital's front gate faces the Mahapalika Marg and its rear gate opens to the Times of India lane between the Azad Maidan Police Station and the Special Branch Office. The Special Branch Office faces the Rang Bhavan Lane at the T-junction. By its side is the Police Dog Squad Office.

The Rang Bhavan Lane which begins from the Special Branch Office ends at the Mahapalika Marg. As you go towards the main road (Mahapalika Marg) on the left are some shanties, an ATM and later the high walls of St. Xavier's College. On the right are a few residential quarters after which is a high rise building. At the junction, on the left is the St. Xavier's College next to which is the Cama Hospital main gate.

After visiting the spot of the incident, we went to the Cama Hospital. The sight of the sharpnel-ridden walls and floors were definitely not for the faint-hearted. My heart went out to the officers and men who had faced the grenades and bullets there that night.

My sister Revati and I met Mr. Sadanand Date, the Additional Commissioner, Central Region who was injured in the grenade attack by the terrorists in the Cama Hospital. Mr. Date and his men had rushed into the Cama Hospital soon after the terrorists fled the CST Railway Station.

He had been badly injured and was still on crutches. This is his story:

He and his men had reached Cama Hospital around 11pm. They were led by a watchman of the hospital to the 6th floor of the building. The two terrorists were already on the terrace. It started with him throwing a metal piece towards the terrace to confirm the presence of the terrorists there. A burst of AK-47 fire came in reply. Later the terrorists also threw some grenades.

Within minutes, a sub-inspector and a constable had been killed. Mr. Date himself sustained grenade sharpnel injuries. He asked the injured constables to go to the casualty ward for treatment and to ask for reinforcements.

After meeting Mr. Date, we met Mr. Hasan Gafoor at his residence. I had carried a book on weapons, which

Ashok had brought from Pune, just three days before 26/11. He wanted to gift it to Mr. Gafoor.

This is what Mr. Gafoor said:

He was not aware as to how Ashok landed up at the Cama Hospital, when he himself had summoned him to the Trident Hotel. He also said that it was Ashok who had shot at and injured the terrorist Kasab with his AK-47. At the rear gate of the Cama Hospital, the terrorists had fired in the direction of Mr. Karkare and the others from the Cama Hospital terrace. Ashok had responded with a burst of AK-47 in the direction of the terrorists.

Mr. Gafoor also disclosed that Kasab had said in his interrogation that this type of fire was indicative of a trained hand and they had thought that a professional team had arrived. This had made them flee from Cama Hospital in a hurry, leaving behind one of their bags. This bag contained a pistol and two AK-47 magazines.

But somehow, beyond a point, Mr. Gafoor appeared unwilling to go into the details. I was disappointed.

In the evening, the lone survivor of the incident, Constable Arun Jadhav accompanied us on our revisit to the spot. This was his story, on that day, as told to me. It appeared natural, spontaneous, from the heart and I could see him living it out as he walked through the spot.

"All the three officers and constables including me reached the rear gate of the Cama Hospital at different timings. Date Sir's gunman Constable Tilekar came out bleeding from the gate. We broke open the gate and got him out. He told us that terrorists were on the terrace. Kamte Sir took the pistol from him. The pistol was jammed with a bullet – he disengaged it.

"Tilekar then informed that Date Sir was injured and was alone upstairs in that condition. They put Tilekar in a vehicle and sent him to the hospital. At that time the terrorists hurled some grenades towards the direction of the rear gate. They also fired at us. Kamte Sir fired back towards the terrorists with his AK-47. After that, I do not know who he was saying it to but I heard him say, 'Call the army, call the army' thrice.

"Before this, the officers had approached the shanties located next to the rear gate. These are the residences of the hospital employees. Just a while ago, one of the residents was killed in the terrorist firing. So the entire neighbourhood had shut the lights and had locked themselves in. We knocked on several doors as Kamte Sir and Karkare Sir wanted to know the exit and entry points of the hospital building. However, there was no help forthcoming. We were also at a disadvantage because the street lights in the lane behind the Cama Hospital had been switched off. It was also pretty dark as it was a new moon day.

"Then, all three of them discussed something for a while. Then they sat inside ACP Pydhonie Sir's Qualis vehicle which had just arrived. Kamte Sir sat in the front seat, next to Assistant Police Inspector Bhosale who was in the driver's seat. Karkare Sir sat in the middle row of this Qualis vehicle. Salaskar Sir and myself along with Kamte Sir's gunmen Jaywant Patil and Yogesh Patil sat behind. At that moment I realised that I had given PSI Alak Noor my spare pistol as he had come without a weapon but I could not see him anywhere.

When we reached near the Special Branch Office, they stopped the vehicle and discussed something amongst themselves. Salaskar Sir got down and took the driver's seat. The vehicle headed towards the Rang Bhavan Lane. When we approached the ATM of the Corporation Bank, suddenly Kamte Sir seemed to have spotted something. Our Qualis screeched to a halt and Kamte Sir turned to his right side, aiming with his AK and immediately fired in that direction. We also fired. The terrorists hiding there returned the fire. I slumped in my seat with the other two constables over me.

"After some time I saw a police vehicle with its beacon light flashing approaching us and I instantly heaved a sigh of relief—I thought it would stop but it just sped past us.

"Minutes later, the two terrorists tried to open our back door but it was jammed. They opened the front doors and removed Salaskar Sir, Kamte Sir and Karkare Sir from the Qualis. They occupied the front seats and began driving. Just then somebody's mobile started ringing. The terrorists fired behind. While driving, Kasab was shaking his hand all the time, writhing in pain. The terrorists got off from the Qualis after some time, somewhere near Mantralaya. After they were gone, I called the Control Room on the wireless and passed on the information."

This preliminary visit and information that we gathered offhand, had thrown light on many of the issues, which had not been clarified till then, by anyone. It was surprising that the investigators in charge, notably the Crime Branch officials had been dithering to give a clear version of what had happened. Especially, when things appeared so simple.

We sought a meeting with the Joint Commissioner of Police, Crime Branch, Mr. Rakesh Maria. Having never met Mr. Maria, I arranged an appointment with him through his wife who was known to me. The meeting was fixed for 10.30 pm at his residence.

I had several unanswered questions plaguing me. I entered Mr. Maria's home – the man in charge of the 26/11 investigation with the expectations of knowing the details of the entire incident as it happened and to bring a closure in my mind. Revati accompanied me.

I asked him, "Since you have interrogated Kasab, could you please tell us what exactly transpired in the Rang Bhavan Lane?"

He replied, "What do you want to know?"

I asked, "What time did the incident take place?"

He replied, "11.50 pm."

I countered, "That's not possible because Ashok's last call on the mobile was at 11.58 pm. This call was answered by Ashok's gunman Jaywant Patil who also died along with Ashok." Mr. Maria kept a straight face.

I went to the next question. "Who shot Kasab?"

Mr. Maria changed his version thrice on the question as to who had shot Kasab. He finally said, "It was only

Ashok who could have shot him and I have said so in the report to the Home Minister."

I requested him to throw light on several issues. Not many seemed to know the exact sequence of events that had taken place before the actual firing. Moreover, not many people knew that Kasab had also been injured in the Rang Bhavan Lane. I requested him to clarify the above issues through a press conference.

Mr. Maria was reluctant. But when I insisted he said "What do you want me to say?"

I said, "Truth. Only the Truth."

He did address such a press conference later, wherein he clarified that it was Ashok who shot and injured Kasab incapacitating him. However, this clarification was given as late as January 10, 2009, when these facts were already known to the Mumbai Police as early as November 27, 2008.

In fact, Mr. A. N. Roy, DG, had in an article written by him in a leading newspaper, confirmed that Ashok had not gone down without a fight. In the article he had stated, "It speaks volumes for his love for his weapon and his deftness with it, that, even when he was caught by surprise by the terrorists that night, he shot at and injured the terrorist, which helped catch him alive later." Then why is it being officially told that the officers sat in a vehicle and were instantly killed?

My final question to Mr. Maria was "How did Ashok go to Cama Hospital when he was initially asked to go to Hotel Trident?"

Mr. Maria replied, "I don't know."

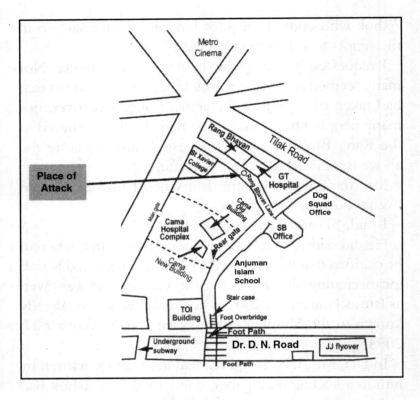

Area Map of Cama Hospital Episode

CHAPTER 5

TRUTH UNFOLDS

The days and weeks that followed were not easy. I had a tough task ahead to unravel what had happened.

Slowly and laboriously, I built up the sequence of events leading to Ashok's arrival near the Cama Hospital. Through my own sources, I managed to procure some of the wireless logs of Ericsson network between South Region Control and the Main Control. I also could secure the logs of the Motorola network; an exclusive network for the senior officers. However, I wanted to be sure and so I requested the Commissioner of Police Mumbai, for the call logs. He simply forwarded my request to the Joint Commissioner of Police (Crime), Mr. Rakesh Maria, for further action. I waited, but there was no further action.

I tried the Right to Information route. The process was long winding and painful. Those efforts merit a story by itself.

I also spoke to a number of eye witnesses. It was

heartening to see so many members of the public coming forward to speak about the incident. There had been many eye witnesses, who had made several calls to the Police Control Room. Strangely and needlessly, a simple and straightforward, tragic but heroic incident was mired in controversy.

At the end of it all, I found my answers. The answers by themselves raised some very important questions.

How did Ashok go out of his jurisdiction?

The Commissioner of Police had called him to Trident Hotel after the mayhem started in South Mumbai.

Ashok also told me this at about 10.45 pm when I called him on his way to Trident.

By the time Ashok was on the road, the situation had considerably deteriorated. Too many things had been happening.

What happened subsequently?

Here are the wireless excerpts:

23 hrs, 11 mins:
East Region (from Ashok's wireless) **to Main Control:** Ask Commissioner of Police as to which spot I am to report to?

23 hrs 13 mins:
Main Control to East Region: I will call and ask.
Control to Police Commissioner: Calling (does not

get through).

23 hrs 16 mins:
Main Control to East Region (Ashok): Please Sir, your present location?
East Region to Control: To reach 10 minutes. To reach Taj in 10 minutes.
Main Control to East Region: Noted Sir.

By this time, apparently, the Jt. CP (Crime), Mr. Rakesh Maria, had taken charge of the Control Room; he was controlling and directing officers, men and resources.

23 hrs, 17 mins:
Main Control to East Region: Crime Sir (Mr. Maria) is asking for your exact location.
East Region to Main Control: Wadala passing, Wadala passing.
Main Control to East Region: Noted Sir.

23 hrs, 22 mins:
East Region to Main Control: Approaching, approaching Zone 1 office.
Main Control to East Region: Understood Sir.
East Region to Main Control: Orders, orders for me.
East Region to Main Control: What are the orders for me?
Main Control to East Region: I will ask Crime Sir (Mr. Maria) and tell you.

It is pretty clear that the operator on line was asking Mr. Maria, who was in charge of the Control Room for orders to be passed on to Ashok. The next excerpts from the wireless logs are revealing. Within two minutes came the response.

23 hrs, 24 mins:
Main Control to East Region: There is an operation going on near S B (Special Branch) office, you come there.

He had received the message and had quickly acted on it as the following wireless exchange shows:

23 hrs, 33 mins:
Main Control to East Region: Firing going on at Cama Hospital and you are to come there.
East Region W.T. (Walkie Talkie) to Main Control: (Ashok's operator answers) East Region Sir has reached Cama Hospital five minutes back.
Control: Noted.

It is so clear. Then why did Mr. Maria deny knowledge of how Ashok went to Cama Hospital? It was he who had directed Ashok there and yet he denied it flatly. Why?

Mr. Karkare in the meantime had reached the CST. The terrorists had just fled the place after the gruesome carnage. People had spotted them running over the Times of India overbridge into the Times of India lane.

Mr. Karkare donned his bullet proof vest, wore his helmet and set out to go after the terrorists, motivating his men. After he reached the lane, he assessed the situation. The following transcript reveals his assessment and strategy:

23 hrs, 24 mins:
Mr. Karkare to Main Control: We are at Cama Hospital. Firing and grenade blasts are going on (in Cama Hospital), 3-4 grenade blasts have taken place in the last five minutes. We need to encircle Cama Hospital. We are near SB 2 office side. Send a team from the front side of Cama Hospital. This needs to be CO-ORDINATED so that there is no crossfiring. Similarly Mr. Prasad who is there – ask him to request the Army for their commandos. We are near SB 2 office, firing going on the 5-6th floor plus three to four grenade blasts heard. Over.

23 hrs, 27 mins:
Main Control to Karkare: Sir, you need help from the front side of Cama. Correct?

23 hrs, 28 mins:
Karkare to Main Control: ATS QRT team is here and so is a Crime Branch team here from the SB2 side. Therefore, we need a team from the front side (of Cama Hospital). We need to ENCIRCLE Cama and SURROUND it. Also tell Mr. Prasad to speak to the army authorities.

23 hrs, 30 mins:
Main Control to Karkare: Noted Sir.

It is so evident. Mr. Karkare was lucid. Very clear about the situation and very specific in his instructions. This was the Anti Terrorist Squad Chief, Maharashtra, giving instructions, during what was by now clear – A Terror Attack.

Let us consider the distances from various points to the front of the Cama Hospital. From the Main Control Room at that hour with no traffic it would have been two minutes. From CST, two minutes. From South Region office, it would have been five minutes.

That no force had reached is certain. Why?

Were Mr. Karkare's instructions ignored?

The Officer requesting was the head of the Anti-Terrorist Squad and the Officer-in-charge of the Control Room was the head of the Crime Branch.

Was it wilful negligence or incompetence?

The fact that the reinforcement did not reach the front of the Cama Hospital is inexplicable.

At about 11.45 pm Inspector Dhurgude arrived near the corner of the St. Xavier's College (on the front side of the Cama Hospital). He saw the two young terrorists walking on the footpath in front of St Xavier's College. The terrorists had jumped out of the front gate of the hospital, with no one to challenge them. Dhurgude confronted them. In reply, they shot him dead at the corner of the Rang Bhavan Lane.

Had Mr. Karkare's instructions been complied with, the two terrorists could have been apprehended at the front gate itself and Dhurgude would not have lost his life. It is quite evident that even after the incident was unfolding inside the Cama Hospital for almost an hour there were no reinforcements at the front gate.

At about the same time, Mr. Maruti Phad, driver of Mr. Bhushan Gagrani, (Principal Secretary, Medical Education), was asked by his boss to reach Mantralaya in case he was required for this emergency. Since Phad resided in the nurses' quarters in the Rang Bhavan Lane, he got into the official Honda City car to proceed towards the Mahapalika Marg when he saw Dhurgude being shot by the terrorists. The very next moment they aimed their guns at him and fired, blowing off one of his fingers. Despite this Phad quickly used the central locking system and began reversing back into the lane. The terrorists came closer to the car and fired again. Phad slumped below his seat, feigning to be dead. Since they could not open the doors of the car, they began walking into the Rang Bhavan Lane.

The Phad family was watching the entire incident from the window of their 11th floor residence. They called the Control Room and asked for help.

Two constables of Azad Maidan Police Station also

witnessed this incident from behind a tree on the opposite side of the Rang Bhavan Lane. They informed South Control accordingly.

23 hrs 48 min
Azad Maidan Peter one to South Control: Firing going in the St. Xavier's lane. Need help.

When we visited the Rang Bhavan Lane, we spoke to a number of residents who had witnessed the entire incident. They had called 100 (which is part of the Control Room) a number of times and provided information about the terrorists moving freely in the lane for over 15 minutes.

In the meantime what did the three Officers do?

After the exchange of fire at the rear gate at about 11.35-11.40 pm, the three officers were huddled in a meeting, planning a strategy. Mr. Karkare had of course called for help to be deployed on the front side of the Cama Hospital. Little did he know that his request had gone unheeded.

Some constables recalled that Ashok in the meantime wanted to assess the resources at hand. He wanted the officers and men to fall in for a head count. But after some discussion they decided that this would not be wise, since making all the officers and men gather at one place would only make them an easy target.

After the last response from the Control Room at 11.33

pm there was no further input to Mr. Karkare and there was a lull of over 15 minutes.

So much had happened, but curiously, there was no word from the Control Room. If there were indeed some communication, that is not reflected in the records made available to us after our RTI application.

There is no indication in all the wireless logs provided to us or which we could access otherwise to say that the three unfortunate officers were informed that the terrorists had entered the lane.

Then why did the officers venture into the lane? All together? And in one vehicle?

It is clear. Mr. Karkare had given a call for rein-forcements to be sent to the front side of the Cama Hospital as early as 11.24 pm, about 35 minutes before.

In any situation, the Control Room is the nerve centre which has an account of all the resources, the authority to move most of the resources and to keep officers on field apprised of what is happening with relevant information. That is because officers at a particular spot do not know of what is happening elsewhere. The idea is to achieve a coordinated response to any challenge and to put the available resources to optimum use.

Sadly in this case, there was not even one response to the earlier call of Mr. Karkare, asking for reinforcements to be sent on the front side. It was not as if the Control Room itself was unaware of the developments. There was enough information from the police and from the locals in the area of the terrorists' movements.

The three officers were aware of the following:
- There had been an exchange of fire at the rear gate.
- This much was certain that the terrorists were inside the Cama Hospital.
- That Addl CP Date and others were trapped inside was also established, by the account given by the injured constable Tilekar.

Constables present at the rear gate of the Cama Hospital have said that it was at about midnight that the three officers sat in the car and headed towards the SB office.

It is evident that after instructing the Main Control Room to send forces to the front side of the Cama Hospital, Mr. Karkare's team had set out to enter the hospital gate from the front side. The motive was clear – one Additional CP was injured and trapped inside, with the terrorists still there.

Mr. Karkare had also left his Motorola walkie-talkie with his operator Mathne at the rear gate so that he could coordinate with the rear of the hospital through Ashok's Motorola.

In the course of my efforts to find out what had happened, I had also spoken to Constable Mathne, the wireless operator of Mr. Karkare. He had categorically said that Mr. Karkare had instructed the constables and officers at the rear gate of the Cama Hospital that he and his team were going to enter the hospital from the front side and they should ensure that there is no crossfire.

The three officers had set out to enter the hospital from the front side expecting reinforcements at the front gate as per Mr. Karkare's directions to the Control Room. They were also not aware that a number of calls to 100 had been made by various people from the lane, informing the police that the terrorists were in the lane.

What was going on the wireless in the meantime?

23hrs 52 min
Main Control to Peter LT Marg: There is a red colored car opposite the St. George's Hospital. The information is that there are three terrorists.
South Control to LT Marg: Calling. There is a red coloured vehicle at St. George's Hospital.

(St. George's Hospital is situated in another direction, 2-3 km away from Cama Hospital.)

00hrs 01min
Control to Peter DB Marg: You have to come to Metro Cinema opposite Metro. There is information that there are three suspected terrorists in a vehicle. It's a red coloured vehicle.
South Control to HO Striking 2: Please send your *amaldar*. There is a red car and there are three terrorists in that.
(Metro is on the main road 1 km away from the SB office.)

It appears that the Officers and their men were opposite the SB office when the 12.01 am message was flashed. It was at this point that Salaskar took the wheel, so as not to leave it to a driver in an emergency.

Why did the three senior officers go together?

Of all the questions raised about the 26/11 incident this probably is the most repeated.

The question arises out of a certain lack of understanding of the police hierarchy and functioning.

The Police Force in a State is headed by the Director General of Police. The Commissioner of Police, Mumbai is of the rank of an Additional DG of Police, then comes the post of IG of Police (Jt. Commissioner in Mumbai), then DIG (Additional Commissioner of Police), then Superintendent of Police (DCP), then Deputy Superintendent of Police (ACP), then Inspector, Sub-Inspector and others.

Mr. Karkare was the head of the ATS and was of the rank of an Inspector General of Police and Ashok was an Additional Commissioner of Police. Mr. Salaskar was an Inspector.

Unlike many uniformed forces, the police functioning is varied. They detect crime, maintain law and order, fight cases in courts, escort prisoners, protect VVIPs and in the extremist affected areas, also fight a war. Mr. Karkare was known for his composed disposition in adverse circumstances and Ashok had fought extremists earlier in Naxalite areas. Mr. Salaskar was adept at the use of

AK-47, but the weapon had been with-drawn from him.

Moreover, in any operational situation in the police, one cannot conceive of a situation where the seniormost officer travels alone with constables.

The situation too was different that night.

With scant inputs and meager resources, Mr. Karkare had to tackle the situation personally. He was on an operation, on way to enter the Cama Hospital Gate from the front side and he could not have been moving only with constables. He had to have the best team with him. It was but natural he took Ashok who was the only officer around with an AK-47 and Mr. Salaskar who was a veteran of many an encounter.

The three officers and their team had set out from the SB office towards the front gate of the Cama Hospital and entered the Rang Bhavan Lane.

It was around 12.03-12.04 am.

What exactly happened? How did it happen?

I have already recounted the account given by Constable Jadhav who was seated in the rear of the Qualis, who miraculously survived the ambush.

But there were also several eye witnesses, who watched everything from their houses.

One account was vivid.

It is a first person account given by a student (name withheld), who resides on one of the higher floors of the Nurses' Quarters in the Rang Bhavan Lane. The window of his bedroom overlooks the very spot where the exchange of fire took place between the terrorists and the three police officers.

"At around 9.30 pm, my father and I were heading towards V T Station to board the Siddheshwar Express to go to Solapur. When we reached the CST at around 10 pm, we heard loud explosions and sound of bullets being fired. People were running out of the station and some of them were jumping from the grill of the boundary wall.

"My father asked the taxi driver to turn around and we rushed back home. I stood near the corner of St. Xavier's College as I had to meet my friend's mom who was to give me something. As soon as I came back to our housing society, I heard of the firings in Taj Hotel and Oberoi. I came home and went up to the terrace. Shortly, I could hear heavy firing in the Cama Hospital. I came down by the lift and I heard my friends say that terrorists had entered our lane.

"I went back home. I heard the loud screeching of a vehicle, so I rushed to look from my bedroom window. All this was happening right under my eyes. I saw a hefty man in a police uniform (Ashok) getting out from the front side seat next to the driver's, taking position and firing towards the bushes. Then there was an exchange of fire – it resembled a string of firecrackers – and then there was silence.

"I saw one terrorist walking in a wayward manner towards the garbage bin, writhing in pain as he kept shaking one of his hands. He was injured. Then the two terrorists went towards the end of the lane near the SB office and fired randomly towards the Dog Squad office. Then they came back towards the Qualis. Just then, I saw a police vehicle with a flashing beacon zooming past the Qualis—it did not stop. Then the terrorists pulled out the people seated in the Qualis and threw them on the road. One of them took the big gun of one of the police officers (AK-47) who was lying there. They drove away.

"The bodies were lying for nearly 40 minutes after which another police vehicle came and took them away."

We had spoken to other residents also who told us that the terrorists spent a good 8-9 minutes in the lane after the incident and that one of the injured terrorists was writhing his hand in pain.

Maruti Phad who had earlier been shot at and injured by the terrorist was still trapped in his car. He watched what was going on in panic. The police Qualis had come to a sudden halt and firing ensued. He recalled that one of the terrorists was injured instantly and dropped the weapon when he was hit again by another bullet.

Which was the police vehicle that went by and who were the officers?

What were they supposed to do on seeing a bullet-ridden police vehicle with shattered windshields with the injured Officers and their men inside?

00.04 to 00.49 – No help arrived for more than 40 minutes after the incident.

The following wireless conversation is an indication:

00hrs 07 min
South Control to Peter D B Marg: Come to GT Hospital. There is *gadbad*.

00hrs09 min
Control to Peter DB Marg: SB gate No. 6, firing noise is going on.
Peter DB Marg to Control: At GT Hospital. Taking a U-turn and going back.
Control to Peter DB Marg: Come from Cama Hospital middle lane (Rang Bhavan Lane).

There is no word whatsoever in response informing the Control Room that there was a Police Qualis which had just been attacked in the lane and that there were several injured inside.

Neither did they stop; nor did they inform.

00hrs13min
Control to Peter DB Marg: Have you reached St. Xavier's?
Peter DB Marg to South Control: I have reached Metro junction and DCP is not allowing us to go ahead.

Not a word though the vehicle had come through the Rang Bhavan Lane.

What can one comprehend of this incident? About the officers who passed by, their sense of duty and courage?

What about the Control Room? And those manning it?

Did they not know that the terrorists were moving unchallenged in the lane for 15 minutes even before the three officers had reached?

What about the Control Room's response after the incident?

Wireless logs reveal a lot.

At around the same time, Ashok's driver had taken the East Region Car (Ashok's car) from the rear of the Cama Hospital to the SB Office and parked it near the Dog Squad Office, oblivious of the firing on the Qualis in the lane. Soon after, at about 12.06 am, the terrorists walked down the lane towards the SB Office and opened fire in the direction of the Dog Squad. Ashok's operator and driver ran for cover. Jarag then called the Main Control at 12.19 am, 12.31 am and 12.37 am, informing them of the incident.

He had specifically mentioned that the car of the East Region (Additional CP) had been fired upon and no one was injured (obviously he did not know that Ashok was already hit earlier down the lane). He had also informed the Control Room that two people had fired on the car and they needed urgent help.

The Control Room did not ask any questions. Even after a senior officer's car had been fired upon, they did not even ask about the whereabouts of the Additional CP, East Region.

Was the Control Room aware of the fate of the

three officers by now?

Members of the public had called 100 from their cell phones. But was there any information on the wireless?

Some wireless transcripts are revealing:

00hrs 04min

Bravo 6 to Main Control: There is sound of firing near SB Office near Gate no 6.

(Note: this was soon after the Qualis carrying Mr. Karkare's team was fired upon).

Main Control to Bravo 6: Understood

(Note: There is nothing to indicate that the Main Control attempted to find out either from Mr. Karkare or Ashok as to what was happening despite knowing they were near S B Office).

00hrs25min

Abel Mobile (Arun Jadhav who survived inside the Qualis) **to Control:** Two terrorists have kidnapped a Qualis car from the Rang Bhavan Lane. PI Salaskar, ATS Sir (Karkare) and South Region Sir (by mistake, he meant East Region) had been fired at...

00hrs33min

Azad Maidan-3 to South Control (while passing hrough the Rang Bhavan Lane): Three people are lying in the St. Xavier's lane. We need a stretcher. (Driver Phad who was lying injured in his car saw this vehicle pass by without stopping at the spot, even as the injured officers lay there).

00hrs40min
Peter LT Marg to South Control: Please send help
to SB Lane. Two, three people are lying injured. I think
it's Kamte Saheb, please send help immediately.

00hrs47min
Karkare's walkie-talkie to Control: Karkare Sir, East
Region Sir and PI Salaskar Sir are injured. We are
taking them to the hospital.

00hrs49min
Peter LT Marg Mobile to South Control: Kamte
Saheb and Salaskar Saheb have been fired upon.
Leaving for GT Hospital.
Abel Pydhonie to South Control: Salaskar Saheb and
Kamte Saheb are injured, we are taking them to GT
Hospital from Rang Bhavan Lane.
(**Note:** 23hrs 24min to 00hrs 49 – No help or rein-
forcements came for 1hr 15mins though Control Room
and South Control are 2-5 minutes away from Cama
Hospital.)

By now, it was clear that those who were on the wireless
network of the Mumbai Police were aware that the three
officers had been attacked and injured.
There were also inputs from the members of the public.
The residents of the Rang Bhavan Lane were desperate.
A number of them made frantic phone calls to the
Control Room at 100. Some called repeatedly. Giving
information, asking for help, describing the terrorists and

even telling the police how to get there.

The efforts of two people stand out.

Their mobile call records show that they called 100 twelve times between 00.02.48 hrs and 00.17.00 hrs.

The call made at 00.02.48 hrs lasted 75 seconds. This was the time the terrorists were moving in the lane, before the three officers had arrived.

Another call at 00.05 hrs lasted 119 seconds. This must have been just after the ambush on the three officers and their men.

The other person called 100 at 00.05.53 for four minutes. He had given a vivid description of what had happened. He had even told the police how the terrorists could be apprehended if they come from both sides of the Rang Bhavan Lane. The terrorists had been moving about around the spot for nearly eight minutes after the incident.

Could the lives of the three Officers have been saved?

These conscientious citizens called before the incident and after, when the three Police Officers were lying on the road for 40 minutes. When after a full forty minutes help arrived, Salaskar was still breathing as he was taken to the hospital. If only help had arrived earlier, Salaskar would certainly have been saved and may be Mr. Karkare and Ashok too. The thought of our husbands lying bleeding for 40 minutes with no help, haunts all our families.

In conclusion, here is a conversation which strangely highlights the fact that Mr. Rakesh Maria who was at the helm of the Main Control Room actually feigned ignorance as late as 1 am about the location of the two officers, Mr. Karkare and Ashok.

The following transcript speaks for itself:

Commissioner of Police (Mr. Hasan Gafoor) calling Mr. Maria on the wireless set:

00hrs56min
Commissioner of Police: The fellows caught at Chowpatty need to be immediately interrogated. Over.

Mr Maria: Noted Sir. There are two fellows Sir, apparently caught at Chowpatty. If you permit me I will bring them to the Crime Branch Sir and will interrogate them here Sir.

Commissioner of Police: Understood. What is the location of Mr. Karkare and Kamte? And what is the situation about Central Region?

Mr. Maria: Sir ... Sir Central Region (Mr. Date) ...Sir is in Cama Hospital... in Cama Hospital Sir and Ashok is near the SB Office Sir. He is covering the SB Office, Sir.

(Note: calls to Control Rooms show that information was passed on at 00.25 am, 00.33 am, 00.40 am, 00.49 am, of them being injured and being moved to the hospital).

Commisioner of Police: What about Mr. Karkare?

Mr. Maria: Sir... Sir he.. he.. he.. Hemant was, Sir, at CST Railway Station, Sir. I will find out the location and tell him to get in touch with you right away, Sir.

(Note: the Control Room call logs show that Mr. Karkare had given his location at Cama at 11.24 pm, 11.27 pm, 11.28 pm and 11.58 pm).

Commissioner of Police: I only want to know whether Mr. Karkare and Kamte are injured or are they safe? And similarly has Central Region got any medical aid and similarly all other injured been provided with medical aid?

Mr. Maria: Sir, trying to do that, Sir. Sir, as for the report... that there was firing on East Region (Ashok Kamte) vehicle nobody is injured but Sir, Central Region I am not able to get through. As soon as I get through I will get back to you.

Police Commissioner: You will send a party to rescue him.

Mr. Maria: Already done, Sir.. Already done, Sir. Additional CP Crime and there are three units of Crime Branch on the job, Sir.
Police Commissioner: Noted, Over.

Where were the teams?

Where was the Additional CP, Crime?

We learnt that one Additional CP with half a dozen armed constables stayed put on the terrace of the Anjuman School (opposite the rear gate of the Cama Hospital) for over an hour till 00.30 am.

Was he not supposed to rescue Mr. Date as informed by Mr. Maria to Mr. Gafoor?

What does he do?

At about 00.25 am Jadhav had informed on the wireless that Mr. Karkare's team had been fired upon in the Rang Bhavan Lane (just about 400 metres away from Anjuman School) and they were injured.

This officer chose to leave the Anjuman School at about the same time and took the opposite direction to exit from the Times of India side, even as the three officers were lying in a pool of blood just about half a kilometre away.

Another Additional CP, it is learnt, was right there in the SB office when Mr. Karkare's team was ambushed in the lane a few hundred feet away.

What was he doing inside? When did he come out?

Some of the constables saw him walk out of the SB

Office after the firing in the Rang Bhavan Lane. Where did he go?

Everyone knew right from 11.05 pm, that Date was in Cama Hospital and yet for over an hour no reinforcements were sent to the front side of the hospital, which is just minutes away from the CP office and the Control Room!

Why? Inefficiency? Incompetency?

Why did Mr. Maria feign ignorance to the Commissioner of Police on Mr. Karkare's location at 00.56 am, when the call logs clearly indicated that the ATS Chief was at Cama rear gate at 11.24 pm and the fact that Ashok and Mr. Karkare were injured?

Why did such a senior officer like Mr. Maria, deny that he had called Ashok to the Cama Hosptial, despite the wireless logs showing this?

Police were stopped at Metro and not allowed to go near Cama Hospital. Cowardice?

A police vehicle passes by the three injured officers without stopping. Ashok was in uniform. Could they have missed them?

Mr. Karkare was very clear in his instructions. Yet the Control Room does not send reinforcements. If they had, even Dhurgude would have been saved.

The Mumbai Police claim that 200 police personnel were sent to Cama Hospital. Where were they ?

Did the Ram Pradhan Committee gloss over these glaring acts of incompetence?

If only Mr. Karkare's team had the benefit of proper briefing from the Control Room on what was happening at the front of the Cama Hospital, the story of that night could have been entirely different.

Mr. Karkare's team managed to injure Kasab, even when they were ambushed. With prior information (which was available with the Control Room), they would have ambushed the terrorists.

And this is what stings my heart.

■

CHAPTER 6

MY TRYST WITH RTI

I always believed that the Police fraternity is a family and issues should be sorted out within that sphere. Instead of the anticipated support from this family, I was faced with unexpected roadblocks at every juncture. It is only because I was denied certain documents that would throw light on the Cama Hospital incident that I had to resort to the Right to Information Act.

This formidable weapon of the common man that has armed him with the right to demand transparency from the government and make it accountable has unfortunately been mocked at in the corridors of the Mumbai Police, as I was to find out.

I had to invoke the RTI even for procuring Ashok's post-mortem report, a certificate so mandatory for various insurance claims. A document that is routinely made available to the family in such circumstances was denied to me. Though saddened, I was now getting accustomed to these hindrances. Every incident strengthened my determination to get to the truth. My initial anger and helplessness had now turned into a steely resolve.

Why was I forced to take the RTI route?

In my efforts my sister Revati, who is a High Court lawyer and her colleague, Shrikant Gavand, helped me.

The following is the chronology of my efforts.

January 28, 2009

I had written a letter to the Commissioner of Police, Mumbai requesting for Ashok's call log records in both the networks – Motorola and Ericcsson. These records would throw light on what had transpired that fateful night.

January 31, 2009

Mr. Hasan Gafoor replied "... the Joint Commissioner of Police, Crime, Mumbai has been directed to take further necessary action in the matter."

Joint Police Commissioner, Mr. Rakesh Maria did not respond.

After I had waited for a month, I finally decided to invoke the RTI Act.

March 4, 2009

I filed an RTI application before the Public Information Officer (Assistant Commissioner of Police, Co-ordination), CP Office and requested for the Call Log records (wireless)—both the written and the audio transcripts.

April 4, 2009

I received a letter from the Assistant Police Commissioner (Co-ordination), designated as Public Information Officer (PIO), rejecting my application. He sought cover under Section 8 (h) of the Act, which states that "information that may impede the process of investigation or apprehension or prosecution of offenders" should not be revealed. He had enclosed a letter of the Joint CP Crime, Mr. Rakesh Maria. It stated, "Please reject the information sought by Mrs. Vinita Kamte under the RTI Act. The information cannot be given to her under Sec 8 (h) of the said Act."

April 29, 2009

I challenged this order before the Deputy Commissioner of Police, the appellate authority.

May 25, 2009

The Appellate Authority, Deputy Commissioner of Police S. M. Sabade observed that the PIO was wrong in rejecting my request for the call logs without application of mind and that he had simply relied on Mr. Maria's letter for rejecting my application. He further observed that the order of rejection does not specify how parting with the information will affect the investigation. Mr. Kamte and the other officers had laid down their lives for the country and to reject Mrs. Kamte's request on such baseless grounds was wrong.

However, in his order he allowed only inspection of the records, not the copies as I had requested.

June 3, 2009

Revati and her colleague went for the inspection. Sub Inspector Mr. Adhale came with the written Call Log records, which were shockingly just loose sheets comprising photostat copies of the written Call Log records. Revati insisted that they would like to inspect original Call Log records. The reply was that the original records had been handed over to the Ram Pradhan Committee and they were assured that these would be procured by June 6.

June 6, 2009

My representatives visited again. The originals were not procured as promised.

June 9, 2009

I wrote to the members of the Ram Pradhan Committee—both Mr. Pradhan and Mr. Balachandran. I stated that, "... it is requested that since the work of the Commission is over, the originals may kindly be sent by the 11th of June, 2009 to the concerned authority so as to enable me/my representatives to inspect the same by the 12th of June."

June 11, 2009

The Committee denied having the originals. Mr. V. Balachandran, member, Ram Pradhan Committee replied by e-mail stating: "... the committee has received only certified copies of the wireless Call Log."

This was shocking. Obviously the Mumbai Police were unwilling to show us the 'original' call logs, for reasons best known to them.

On the same day, I wrote a letter to the CP and the Joint CP L&O (Mr. K. L. Prasad) pointing out the above.

June 12, 2009

Mumbai Police sought time to seek legal opinion on Mr. Sabde's order granting inspection of the Call Logs.

July 7, 2009

Mr. Prasad communicated that they had sought legal opinion and accordingly the information could be 'parted with.' But somehow it was interpreted to mean that we can only 'peruse' the records and not take copies of either the documents or the audio tapes.

July 20, 2009

I wrote to Mr. K. L. Prasad stating very clearly that while I will go ahead with the inspection, I still reserve my right to go in appeal to procure the records.

Jul 29 and 30, 2009

On both these days my representatives went for inspection and yet were not shown the originals. Even the audio CD which was shown had been created on the 6th of January, nearly a month and a half after the incident; obviously not the original recordings.

During these inspections, we also made a request for the details of recordings of the calls made to the number

100.

We were flatly refused and were told to make a separate application for these, despite the fact that the request was part of all the requests which we had made and which were upheld by the Appellate Authority

Aug 04, 2009

I filed a separate application seeking call log records, written and audio, made to 100 on the night of November 26, 2008. This was rejected on September 4 on flimsy grounds and I have gone in appeal, which is pending.

Aug 21, 2009

We filed a second appeal to the State Chief Information Commissioner, Maharashtra, Dr. Suresh Joshi, seeking the original copies of the Call Logs, both written and audio.

Oct 15, 2009

The State Chief Information Commissioner, Mumbai allowed my appeal and directed the Police to hand over the copies of the written and audio records of Call Logs within 30 days.

My patience and determination had paid off. Coming from a family of lawyers and being a lawyer myself, I was more than familiar with the system and was confident that I would get the necessary information.

I must mention here that the RTI is one of the most effective legislations of recent times. My personal experience has taught me that without this piece of legislation, it is impossible for the common man to get to the truth.

I know that I do not have to rely on persons in position for the rightful information. I have a powerful tool in my hand, the RTI. The route may be long and tardy but truth will ultimately prevail.

There were still questions.

Why were they reluctant and obstinate to show me the originals? I was to find answers in a different way, soon.

Ram Pradhan Committee Report

The Ram Pradhan Committee was a two member, high level committee constituted in December to enquire into the incidents of the terrorist attack on 26/11 and identify lapses if any. Pursuant to a statement made by Mr. Jayant Patil, State Home Minister, on news channels that the Ram Pradhan Committee would look into my allegations (of lapses in the Cama Hospital incident), I wrote to the Committee on Jan 27, 2009, stating that I would like to appear before it.

Mr. Ram Pradhan called and informed me that they were not empowered to call any members of the public as their terms of reference were limited. Thereafter, I wrote to Mr. Jayant Patil on Feb 6, 2009 requesting him to widen the terms of reference, if required so as to enable me to appear before the Committee. Unfortunately, I received no response to the same.

It is surprising to note that the persons on whom the Ram Pradhan Committee relied were mostly persons who were themselves interested in covering up their lapses. ∎

CHAPTER 7

RIOTS AND BATTLES

MUMBAI POSTING

Ironically, it is in Mumbai that Ashok had his first taste of sub-standard equipment provided to the Police Force during his tenure as DCP, Zone I in South Mumbai in 2000-2002. And it was in 2008 in this very place that the night of Mumbai terror raised doubts on the quality of the bullet-proof jacket worn by Mr. Hemant Karkare.

Ashok was posted twice in this metropolis – as Deputy Commissioner of Police (DCP) Zone I, in South Mumbai in 2000 and then as Additional Commissioner, East Region in June 2008.

Some incidents shook Ashok's confidence in the powers-that-be, about their intentions and of their concern for the safety of the force.

Polyfibre batons were newly introduced into the Mumbai Police when Ashok was posted as DCP Zone I. He had to lathi-charge in the Mantralaya incident after riots broke out following the No Confidence Motion won by the Vilasrao Deshmukh Government. Much to

Ashok's chagrin, in the lathi charge, his new *lathi* broke into two. The *lathis* of some of his policemen also broke into several pieces during that crucial police action. Distressed with this occurrence, that could have put the rioters at an advantage and made policemen vulnerable to their ire, Ashok wrote to the concerned authority about the *lathis* being of sub standard quality. He also mentioned that such poor quality equipment could put the life of policemen in danger. As a sample, he enclosed his broken *lathi*. Later, the *lathis* were replaced with better quality ones. That it required a rioting incident to expose the sub-standard quality, surprised him.

In another incident, Ashok as a member of a committee for the procurement of bullet-proof jackets visited the Naigaum Police Headquarters to test them. He tested the bullet proof jackets by actually firing at them with different weapons from different distances. At the end of the testing Ashok's findings were concrete. He reported "The jacket tested is sufficiently strong to resist penetration by conventional hand guns firing conventional and standard ammunition (issued to police). It cannot be said for certain that the jacket can ensure safety against sub-machine guns at normal close quarter combat range of 25-30 yards firing on full automatic. It may also be kept in mind that the maximum velocity of round tested was 1280 feet/second as higher velocity ammunition was not available." (In short this means that these jackets can just about withstand small arms fire but cannot withstand automatic weapons of higher velocity like AK-47 (velocity more than 2100 ft/sec from a range of 25-30 yards, not to speak of shorter distances). I cannot say if these were the same bullet-proof jackets that were used on the night of 26/11. However, when Mrs. Karkare recently made a request under the RTI for a copy of the *panchanama* of the bullet proof jacket worn by Mr. Karkare, the reply given was, "The bullet-proof jacket is untraceable."

Ashok worked with utmost dedication and courage of conviction. He used to be frustrated at times though, at the political interference in the working of the police force and even sought a transfer. In 2001, he was literally driven up the wall and requested immediate transfer to the Indo-Tibet Border Police. This was a sequel to Medha Patkar's agitation, which she spearheaded for the rehabilitation of families to be affected by the Narmada Dam Project. She had come with a large number of her followers and had congregated at Azad Maidan in South Mumbai. At that time, Ashok was DCP, Zone I and this area was in his jurisdiction. She had threatened to agitate on the road and provoked her followers to do so. Ashok prevailed upon her not to stage the *rasta roko* as it would inconvenience thousands of commuters. He had offered to fix an appointment with the Minister concerned, along with some of her delegates where she could address her grievances. Medha Patkar though seemed in a defiant mood. Ashok then told her in no uncertain terms that if she and her followers took the law in their hands and created public nuisance, he would be forced to take necessary action that would be required to bring the situation under control.

For most of the day, the scenario was quite peaceful as the crowd restricted itself to the Azad Maidan ground. At 5 pm, Mumbai's peak hour for vehicular traffic, Patkar along with her followers suddenly came to one of Mumbai's busiest roads and blocked it. Ashok rushed to the spot and before that asked for reinforcements in the form of empty police vans and women constables as there were at least 100 women agitators. Ashok then tried to call some of his senior officers to apprise them of the situation and to seek appropriate orders but they were out of contact. When he tried to call the Minister concerned, he too was unavailable.

The heart of Mumbai faced chaos as Patkar's *rasta roko* had held up traffic which blocked the roads for several kilometers. With thousands of stranded, angry commuters and hundreds of defiant agitators, it was a situation threatening to get out of control. Ashok never hesitated to take action when it was required to restore peace. His conviction to do the right thing however volatile the situation was, always helped him to be in charge.

He instructed his policemen to clear the road, by physically removing the agitators who were squatting there. Accordingly, many people were arrested and brought to the Azad Maidan Police Station.

Medha Patkar was taken into police custody. She subsequently complained, stating that she had been arrested despite apprising the police that she had a back problem. While the situation was commendably brought under control within half an hour, later during the evening, Ashok's senior called up and expressed displeasure over the action and said that it may have serious consequences. Ashok firmly replied that he had tried to call up the senior before the action but his mobile was switched off. He, being in the field of action did what should have been done to restore order to the mayhem.

At around 10.30 pm, Ashok was asked by his seniors to release Patkar from jail. Disheartened that the authorities had wilted under political pressure, he came to the office the next day and put up his application requesting transfer on deputation to I. T. B. P. (Indo-Tibetan Border Police). The issue simmered for five days, before Ashok was convinced by his superiors to stay on in Mumbai.

In July 2002, the Vilasrao Deshmukh Government won the vote of confidence. As a consequence, supporters of the then opposition leader Narayan Rane and the supporters of the ruling Congress-NCP alliance came face to face opposite the Mantralaya. Within 10 minutes, a motorcycle had been burnt. There were pitched battles on the road. Ashok who was at the spot, brought the situation quickly under control. He had used tear gas shells after a lathi charge and before that he had cautioned some prominent politicians who were at the scene to move away lest they get injured. Later, one of them recollected, with appreciation, Ashok's professionalism towards his job.

The post of DCP of Zone I in Mumbai is one of the toughest for any DCP in Mumbai. It has the Assembly, the Secretariat, several five-star hotels, embassies and residences of VIPs. The Azad Maidan and Mantralaya areas in the Zone are frequent venues for *morchas* and agitations. The brunt of the work is normally taken by the DCP, who in Mumbai is the cutting edge officer.

During his tenure, Ashok dealt with all the law and order situations in his jurisdiction with tact when necessary and firmness when warranted. Despite this, he did not ignore the crime scene. In his tenure, he was involved in as many as nine encounters in which members of the underworld were dealt with.

That Ashok was always relied upon when it came to tough situations was highlighted, during his tenure as Additional Commissioner, East Region, Mumbai.

MNS Chief Raj Thackeray was arrested in November 2008 at Ratnagiri and was being brought to the Bandra Court in Mumbai, on the order of the Court. This was a sequel to the attack on non-Maharashtrians who had come to Mumbai to appear for the Railway Board examination. When news spread that Raj Thackeray was to be produced at the Bandra Court, there were Statewide protests and his followers began making a beeline to Mumbai from several parts of Maharashtra. As Mr. Raj Thackeray's convoy neared Mumbai it had become large and unmanageable. The police along the route from Ratnagiri to Mumbai were unwilling to take the strong action of breaking the convoy. It was left to Ashok through whose jurisdiction the convoy was entering Mumbai. He immediately ordered a *nakabandi* through the route and ordered that the supporters should be stopped from coming into Mumbai. Thackeray himself however, was accompanied by a large crowd. Ashok stood near the barricades at Chembur Naka and soon after letting the police party with Thackeray through, closed the road with barriers and did not allow the rest of his supporters to enter. Ashok, in fact, was blunt to one of the junior officers who escorted Thackeray. He asked, "Why didn't you break the convoy in your area? Are you afraid of not getting a good posting in case he becomes the Chief Minister?"

However, in Bandra, the scenario was the complete reverse. Crowds had begun congregating in large numbers near the Bandra Court. Soon, they began setting buses on fire and the situation became uncontrollable. This area was beyond Ashok's jurisdiction but the Commissioner of Police asked Ashok to move to the troubled area. Ashok was hesitant as he did not want to step into a colleague's jurisdiction. When he expressed this concern to the Commissioner of Police, the latter was firm and ordered, 'Go and take charge.' So, he proceeded ahead. At the Dharavi corner, the policemen tried to stop him, warning him of the violent situation there. Ashok brushed them aside saying that it was for this very reason that he had been sent here. He reached the spot, took charge, ordered firm action and within less than an hour, brought the situation under control—one which had gone out of hand for several hours before.

Ashok did not lose his verve or enthusiasm even as an Additional Commissioner of Police.

I remember one Sunday, we were having lunch at a restaurant in South Mumbai. He got a call from one of his constables that riots had broken out after a local cricket match in Chembur between two groups of a neighbourhood. The area of trouble was the BMC Colony where a 90 feet wide road divides the two communities. Ashok, left his lunch half-way and rushed to the spot. The situation was tense.

The flashpoint had reached when a door of a place of worship was stoned. As the area had a mixed population of both communities, the situation got only worse. A mob of 500 was on its way to block the Eastern Express Highway. When Ashok reached there, his policemen were also being attacked with stones and glass bottles. Ashok immediately lathi-charged the crowd and crippled its movement by hurling tear gas shells. Within minutes the situation came under control and it remained peaceful thereafter.

Ashok was always known for his presence of mind and his outstanding courage to immediately nip in the bud any rioting situation before it went out of control.

In spite of pressures incidental to his job, Ashok loved his profession and pursued it with utter passion. The skirmishes with the powers-that-be did not reduce his faith in the profession. He remained an idealist. His mother says that since childhood, Ashok never showed his emotions to others – he was a very reserved person. She reminisces though, "The only day he danced with joy was when he got the news that he had been selected for the IPS. He came home so unusually happy and excited and literally lifted me up." In fact, during the Civil Services interview he was asked why he did not opt for the IAS, he answered that he would like to be where the action was and hence the IPS was his first choice.

He lived for it. He died for it.

■

CHAPTER 8

SALUTES FROM SOLAPUR

SOLAPUR POSTING

"The last time that the city of Solapur in Maharashtra plunged into grief was after the assassination of the then Prime Minister, Mrs. Indira Gandhi, in 1984. The next time it happened was on the night of November 26, 2008. I saw the same anguish spread like wildfire throughout the city after we got to hear of Ashok's death," my friend in Solapur told me.

She continued, "Even as the residents of Solapur came to terms with this irreparable loss, photographs of Ashok were put up at public chowks and were lined along the roadsides. Business establishments voluntarily downed their shutters and the streets wore a deserted look. People gathered in their neighborhood to pay tributes. Their hero, who had transformed their city into a law abiding and peace loving one in his tenure of 22 months as the Police Commissioner, was suddenly no more."

For the first time in my life I was able to witness in Solapur from close quarters the incredible adulation

Ashok received from the public. His tenure as DIG, Special Protection Unit, an outfit in Pune which trains police officers to protect VIPs, was cut short to one year. The State Government decided to appoint a tough cop to restore sanity to the crime-ridden and riot-stricken Solapur. Ashok was chosen for the post.

In order not to disturb Rahul and Arjun's education in Pune, Ashok decided to move alone to Solapur. His loneliness was somewhat compensated by his affectionate staff and close friends. He had a very talented cook, who, besides dishing out tasty food, was also quick to learn some of Ashok's favourite items, which I taught her in due course of time.

The official residence of the Police Commissioner was a picturesque colonial era bungalow. The bungalow was rather huge for a forced bachelor. When I visited him for the first time after he took charge, I found that he was using just one of the bedrooms while the rest of the house remained deserted. I decided that a warm living room would make him feel more relaxed after a hard day's work. The ceiling of the living room, like all the other rooms was high – about 30 feet, on which was fixed a hundred-year-old chandelier. I brought his grandfather's heritage Venetian tapestry from Pune and draped one of the walls with it. I decorated the other walls with Egyptian paintings and cushioned the floor with Tibetan carpets which we had brought during our Bhandara posting and brightened the cane sofa set with colourful seat and cushion covers. The music system was also fixed, as music was Ashok's passion—he had a fabulous collection of Western music which he had acquired over the years from college days through his various postings including the one in Bosnia. Soon it became his favourite place where he relaxed along with his Basset hounds Hazel and Hillary.

I visited him every fortnight. It was a beautiful bungalow. The dining room and the bedrooms too were spacious and the garden at the rear added to the leisurely feel. The well manicured lawn had a charming sit-out. Here, Arjun, Rahul, Ashok, his friends and I would spend hours playing cricket with the orderlies or just chatting. I was happy that the staff pampered him with their rustic meals. Constable N. Chamke told me that he loved '*kadak bhakri*' (a kind of Indian bread made of jowar or bajra) and '*mirchi cha techa*' (pungent chilly chutney) and '*appe*' (dumplings made out of rice and urad dal, a typical dish from Karnataka).

I was relieved that he was being looked after so well. The staff would often recount to me how Saheb would chat with them after work, enquiring after their families and well-being. Once he called the women sweepers on duty at his bungalow and enquired about their salaries. It was Rs. 250 a month each, and they had to work elsewhere as domestic help to supplement their meagre incomes. Ashok was disturbed to hear this figure and within a short time increased it to Rs. 1,000 per month. The women were moved by this gesture.

Solapur City is in South West Maharashtra, on the border of Karnataka with an area of just 25 square kilometers. It has a population of approximately 14 lakhs with an uneasy mix of various communities—*Dalits* and Upper Castes as well as Muslims. The city has a history of caste and communal trouble, making it a perpetual hotbed for riots. Solapur had seen a deterioration in the law and order situation in the recent years before Ashok took over in 2006. Constables would tell me how stoning policemen on duty, attacking police stations and damaging public vehicles—all at the slightest provocation —was routine. The police force here was a demoralised lot. In addition to their other woes were the indiscriminate suspensions of the constabulary, at the whims and fancies of the superiors. The local *goondas* ruled different areas of the city, unleashing terror through extortion, violence and gang rivalries.

When Ashok took over the reins in August 2006, the city hardly reacted. Most of them did not even know where the official headquarters of the Police Commissioner were located. However, he evoked second glances and became the talk of the town for his shining pate and 'foreigner' looks.

It was not surprising that like in other places where he was posted, in Solapur too Ashok quickly attained the reputation of a tough officer and restored law and order with an iron hand within a few weeks.

I still vividly recall a Sunday morning. It was about half past eight in the morning and Ashok was constantly on the phone. His inspectors were briefing him on a particularly sensitive *Navratri* procession, where some off-duty constables who were part of some *mandals*, were not allowing others to proceed. The entire procession had come to a standstill and the local officers were unable to control them. Finally, with the situation threatening to get out of hand, Ashok reached the spot himself. The constables in the procession were summoned to the nearest police station for 'talks.' There, in the presence of all the officers and men, they got the 'tough' message. Officers who tried to come in the way too got a taste of it. Of course, the problem was instantly solved, the procession moved. It was a lesson well-learnt for times to come—when you are a policeman, you should be unbiased and professional, on or off duty.

That was to be just the tip of the iceberg, though. The city witnessed the power and commitment of this no-nonsense Police Officer within weeks.

On September 29, 2006 Ashok was in Delhi when state-wide incidents of violence were sparked off in the immediate aftermath of the infamous Khairlanji rape and massacre case. He was immediately called back to the city. As he neared the city's outskirts, he called up his constable and asked him to bring his uniform, boots and baton to the Puna Naka (the toll station outside the city), as he always chose to be in uniform and never ever went in his civilian dress when on duty. That was his trademark. When his car reached near the Naka, he changed into his uniform in the vehicle itself and was all set to take charge of the situation.

In the chilling massacre at Khairlanji, four members of a *Dalit* family had been brutally raped and killed in an allegedly planned conspiracy by the upper caste community of the village. A mob had entered the house to carry out this heinous act. Although Khairlanji was located in Bhandara district, anger and unrest spread throughout Maharashtra. Solapur being always extra-sensitive, it was only expected that riots would break out here too. Citizens feared a repeat of the earlier riots and predictably enough, thousands of agitators took to the streets, with swords, sickles and chilli powder to vent their anger.

In 2002, Solapur had witnessed Hindu-Muslim riots and nine people had been killed in police firing. That those deaths had not put any fear in the minds of the people became evident enough with a mob numbering about 10,000 gathering at the Chhatrapati Shivaji Chowk, one of the premier traffic junctions in Solapur. The situation was emotionally and physically charged.

Ashok had barely a dozen policemen to handle the crowd. Much to the amazement of the agitators who until then had bristled with confidence, their new Police Commissioner simply stood facing them with a baton in his hand, a pistol at his waist and a helmet on his head. For the first time in the history of Solapur, the enraged crowd was overawed by the uniform although they had come fully prepared to unleash violence. Perhaps it had something to do with Ashok's powerful personality. Nevertheless, the leaders gave a full-blooded cry and urged their followers to attack.

Ashok gauged the situation in a split second and decided to quell it before it was even triggered off. In a fraction of a moment, as the policemen present on that day recollect, he lifted his baton in a backward forceful swing and with lightening speed, surged his athletic body forward and lathi-charged the leaders with all his might. He instructed the constables to similarly attack the leaders' cronies who were leading the mob. This swift movement took the crowd by complete surprise, used to as it was to hurling stones at the police rather than taking a beating themselves. The hangers-on were shocked and frightened to see their leaders injured.

Within ten minutes the entire crowd dispersed. The agitators had taken to their feet in such a nervous and hurried manner that the *chowk* now resembled a roadside *chappal* bazaar since most of them had fled and left their footwear behind. Solapur was simply stupefied—never in its history had it seen a policeman's baton actually work and make trouble-makers run for their lives. Ashok had instantly become a hero.

On that fateful day of the post-Khairlanji crisis when Solapur underwent a miraculous transformation, Ashok and his men then moved forward towards the Employment Chowk, about 500 metres away from where he had just wielded his *lathi*. Here he saw a huge group of around 1,500 people making their way to the Chhatrapati Shivaji Chowk, apparently unaware of what had transpired there. Ashok decided to cripple their movements. He used a barrage of tear gas shells which sent them scurrying helter-skelter.

The then deputy RTO Mr. Madane who had asked for transfer in a week's time of his joining, was surprised to see the images of Police Commissioner Ashok Kamte dispersing the crowd with his baton without even having to brandish his pistol. Newspapers were flooded with reports that hailed Ashok for his courage and superb skills of riot management. Mr. Madane called up the Collector and said, "Sir, I have decided to stay back in Solapur for the law has come on the road and order is sure to follow." Ashok became synonymous with the rule of law, and local *goondas,* who personified lawlessness, were soon rendered powerless.

Thereafter, curfew was clamped on Solapur city for seven days. Local *goondas* were hunted out from their homes during the night hours and arrested. Some of them were admonished at public *chowks.* Most of the criminals ran away from the city for months on end to escape arrest. During the days of the curfew, Ashok was always in the lead, patrolling the streets almost all hours of the day or night. Solapur's residents just couldn't believe what they saw—a senior IPS officer doing the rounds himself instead of holding fort from the security of his office. Solapurkars soon got used to seeing their Police Commissioner eating bananas and sharing meals with his police teams. Ashok would return home only for a bath and change of clothes and would be back on the road. This he did for the entire week and lost seven to eight pounds at the end of it.

Ashok's subordinates called me up to say that I should be with Ashok to take care of him since the situation was stressful. I rushed to Solapur, worried that Ashok may have over-exerted himself. I stayed for about a week by which time peace had returned to Solapur once again and Ashok was able to get back to his normal routine.

One of the side stories of the entire episode was very interesting and of particular relevance to women.

During the curfew hours, citizens were restrained from stirring out after sunset till early morning. At that time, the Marathi film *'Saatchya Aat Gharat'* (Home Before 7 PM) had been released. It became extremely popular due to the relevance of its title. The story was about the rape of a young college girl. However, women in Solapur used this title to point out how their men, who were regular drunkards were forced to return before nightfall. This was because the liquor dens and permit rooms were not allowed to conduct their usual business. Ashok was thanked by many a wife for having forced men to mend their ways. Ashok became *'Dada'* (elder brother) to all Solapurkars.

After having the anti-social elements on the run during the curfew week, Ashok also got the illegal encroachments removed. He then urged the Municipal Commissioner Mr. Devnikar that this was the opportune time to bring down all illegal political hoardings. When Mr. Devnikar hesitated to do so, Ashok convinced him saying, "At other times you need the *bandobast* of the police to remove these encroachments but now with curfew having been clamped, no local politician or his sycophants will dare to interfere with this action." Around 400-500 trucks of hoardings and encroachments were removed and dumped outside the city in no time. The city wore a neat and clean look once again. And there was not even the slightest whimper of protest.

Solapurkars had by now seen the tough streak in their

Police Commissioner, but very soon were to witness his softer and sensitive side too. Mr. Madane later recalled that during the curfew, people arriving at the Solapur bus stand or railway station faced tremendous inconvenience since no mode of transport was available. Ashok had requested the District Collector to arrange for a shuttle service by taking the help of the Solapur Municipal Transport so that none of the passengers would be stranded. The Collector gave the responsibility to the Road Transport authorities.

Deputy RTO Mr. Madane, who was also a Manager of the city's public transport service, called up Ashok and said, "I have no problem about arranging for buses but what if they get stoned or are set on fire? Can you ensure us protection?" Ashok immediately promised him two police recruits and two escort vehicles per bus. Such kind of support encouraged the RTO to cooperate and the shuttle service became a huge success. Police vehicles also arranged to pick up citizens who wanted to reach the bus stand or railway station or wanted to go to a hospital for any medical emergency. These were always escorted by police personnel to avoid any untoward incident. This humane concern to solve the common man's problems, struck a chord in every Solapurkar's heart.

Thereafter, when desecration of the Ambedkar statue in Kanpur took place and Mumbai and the rest of Maharashtra burnt, not a single untoward incident occurred in Solapur. After all, the city had just recently witnessed their new Police Commissioner's iron hand in the aftermath of the Khairlanji episode.

Ashok became a household name and began to be revered. One day Ashok got a request from a corporator whose son had been hospitalised for a critical illness and had just regained consciousness. "Can you please visit my son?" the father requested. Ashok obliged. The moment the young patient saw Ashok, he jumped from his bed and touched his feet, not even caring about the saline tube injected into his hand.

People recount another incident that showed his popularity. A crowd of about 15,000 people had gathered for a live musical programme to be presented by noted artists of Maharashtra at the city stadium. Prior to the actual programme, the organisers had decided to felicitate local officials and politicians. The audience wasn't too interested and hardly bothered to pay any attention while this formality was being carried out on the stage. It was then Ashok's turn to be honoured. The moment he stepped on to the stage, the audience stood up as one and welcomed him with a thunderous round of applause. The stadium reverberated with clapping and whistling for more than five minutes.

I felt a deep sense of pride when I saw the impact he had on the city. Many homes kept his photograph along with the deities in their homes. Calendars were printed with his photograph and he was fondly called 'Kamte Uncle' by children. Students made scrap books of news items and photographs of Ashok. People would actually throng outside his official bungalow just to have a glimpse of him. When he went to public functions, people would touch his feet. When he was present for security reasons at the functions of political bigwigs, people would mob Ashok instead, much to his embarrassment. The people simply loved their hero, Ashok.

The fact that the smallest of incidents was paid attention to by Ashok can be exemplified by what Sanjay Mhetre, a social worker narrated. A teenage girl was being regularly harassed by a bunch of eve-teasers. While not mustering up enough courage to go and meet 'Kamte Uncle,' she began to pray to a calendar with Ashok's photograph on it. Such was the faith that Ashok had inspired in Solapur. When her father came to know of the matter, he sought an appointment with Ashok who called them both to the office. Soon enough, Ashok sent his men to straighten out the eve-teasers. This also helped send a strong signal in Solapur that the police was in no mood to tolerate any kind of unlawful activity.

On August 16, 2007, in an unprecedented incident, which reverberated in the Maharashtra Legislative Assembly, Ashok arrested Ravikant Patil, a three-time MLA from the Indi segment in Bijapur district. Though Patil represented Indi, a Karnataka Assemly constituency, he lived in Solapur which bordered his constituency. The manner in which Ashok taught Patil a lesson left the Solapurkars mesmerised. It also showed that Ashok was not the kind to get cowed down by those who flaunted their political power. His faith in his uniform and conviction of duty empowered him with this strength. I was proud of my husband for this.

The notorious politician was celebrating his birthday

with friends and cronies and was bursting firecrackers close to midnight at his residence.

A patrolling police party stopped by and requested him to stop disturbing others in the locality and pointed out that a Supreme Court ruling disallowed any loud noise after 10 pm. Ravikant's men refused to pay heed. A police inspector therefore visited Ravikant and asked him to stop the ruckus. The inspector was assaulted by Ravikant's men. Ashok had been keeping tabs on this situation on the wireless from his residence. Soon, he heard calls for reinforcements from the officer at the spot. Sensing trouble, he decided to go himself. On reaching Ravi Patil's bungalow, Ashok could sense that the situation was not exactly under control. He asked the MLA and his cronies to court arrest. An argument ensued. Then there was a minor scuffle, in which Ashok's badge was dislodged. Ashok then pulled Ravikant into the police vehicle. Ravikant's men had by then taken to their heels. When Ravikant was produced before the Magistrate after his arrest, he was brought on a stretcher. On his complaint of 'high-handed behaviour' by Ashok, the latter's reply was that "no one is above the law." This incident reverberated throughout Maharashtra and had its echo in the Assembly session wherein an inquiry was ordered into the incident and some of the politicians clamoured for his transfer. Ashok though was quite unrepentant. He had told the Home Minister that he had done nothing wrong and being transferred was the least of his worries. He had done what he thought was right, it was now up to them to do what they thought was right. Simple and straightforward thinking—like the man himself. Ashok was an uncomplicated and transparent human being and so were all his actions.

The entire episode of the MLA's arrest left an indelible mark on the people of Solapur. They put up huge hoardings of Ashok across the city, depicting him as their hero. One of the slogans read, *"Kamte saab ka danda, Solapur thanda"* (Solapur has cooled off thanks to Kamte Sir's baton). Scooters, autorickshaws and cars carried stickers of Ashok's photographs. One of them wanted to register his scooter with the number AK-47 as Ashok's mastery of the weapon was well-known. Amazingly, he did manage to get this number because at that very time the registration of vehicles in Solapur was being carried out under the AK series. With much amusement, I also gathered that young girls had pictures of Ashok on their mobile phones.

When it was rumoured that he was to be transferred, an 80-year-old woman came to meet him at his official residence. In her *'batwa'* (a home-made purse) she was carrying news clippings of Ashok. She had come all the way to tell him that she was praying hard so that he would not be sent out of Solapur.

By now, Ashok's reputation was enough to instill fear in the minds of the criminals. A small *dhaba* owner, who had often been at the receiving end of some local *goondas* making merry without paying and even forcing him to make financial contributions for one event or the other, plastered his roadside eatery with calendars that had Ashok's photograph printed on them. The *goondas* got the message and never troubled him thereafter. As acknowledgement of all that he had done for Solapur, Ashok was honoured with the 'Solapurkar of the Year' award instituted by *Sakaal*, a widely read vernacular daily of Maharashtra.

Despite his busy schedule, Ashok found time for sports and physical fitness too. He equipped the Police Head-quarters with a gymnasium and had fitness equipment installed at home too. Every evening between 6 and 8 pm, he would be in one of the two gymnasiums. He started the Polly Umrigar Cricket Tournament on August 10, 2007 to commemorate the foundation day of the Solapur Police Commissionerate. Police teams from all over the district took part. The tournament has been renamed as Shahid Ashok Kamte Polly Umrigar Cricket Tournament.

Ashok made a few friends in Solapur with whom he used to spend time in the evenings. However, they recall that partying for Ashok was like a recess between work schedules. Yatin Shah, one of Solapur's leading indus-trialists and his good friend, used to often remark, "I could almost see the transformation in his personality the moment the party got over, the disposition on his face would become stern as soon as he got into the car. In fact, many a time, he would abruptly cut short a party in case of any law and order problem, even if it was minor."

Another friend, Col. Sanjay recalled a particular incident. "Ashok had come to my house in the evening and just a few minutes later he received a phone call that an arch which was being erected for a public function had collapsed at around 10 pm and two people were trapped under it. Ashok immediately asked for his uniform to be brought from the car, quickly changed and rushed to the site."

Ashok's Solapur tenure came to an end and he was transferred to Mumbai as Additional Commissioner, East Region on June 16, 2008.

Remembrances

Shyamrao Dighavkar, Deputy Commissioner of
Police, Solapur

He was the rarest of rare officers who led from the front. He reinstated a number of suspended constables. That was because he believed in quick decisions, and not in prolonged departmental enquiries which led to loss of precious man-hours. The constabulary was grateful to him for this. He brought peace to Solapur, beyond the expectations of people and was therefore God to them. Earlier, the police was trapped between a listless civic administration and an inimical attitude of people towards it. All that changed quite miraculously. He gave back his men the confidence of being effective law enforcers. The civic administration too cooperated to make the city more disciplined. All the local *dadagiri* came to an end. Kamte Sir was Solapur's biggest *dada*.

Sanjay Jadhav, City Reporter, *Sakaal*

He was quick to act and possessed a charismatic personality. This made him the peoples' hero. He brought the city to order within a fortnight of taking charge. The citizens were spellbound. They had never experienced such discipline in the past. When the *Sakaal* newspaper awarded him the 'Solapurkar of the Year' award he said that he dreamt of a "beautiful Solapur city." He loved the city and made it his mission to keep it peaceful. Solapurkars who were traditionally used to even violating curfew norms, realised for the first time, what a real curfew was all about. Kamte Sir would go around the city ensuring that no one broke the law.

He always treated his constables with respect and shared meals with them from the food packets given to the police during curfew hours. When my deputy editor called me up on that fateful night to say that Kamte Sir had been killed in action, I literally froze. I had gone to sleep and therefore not seen the news on TV myself. He asked me to dictate on phone details of his Solapur tenure for the next day's edition. So shocked was I that my hands didn't stop trembling for 15 minutes after that.

Nagnath Chamke, Assistant Sub Inspector, Anil Pore, Police Constable, Vijay Pawar and Apparao Satarkar, Police Naiks

Kamte Sir was so strict that during the curfew, he did not even issue passes to the Mayor or the other politicians of the city. Everyone, no matter what his or her status was, had to abide by the law. He would often point to a cop's *lathi* and say that it should be used to bring order. "It has not been issued to dry clothes on," he would remark in jest. His reputation had reached out to all corners of the district and he would often be invited as a special guest for public functions from all over the district, not just Solapur city.

A lady once came all the way from Akkalkot to meet Kamte Sir to settle her land dispute problem. Kamte Sir politely explained that it was not in his jurisdiction and that she should go and meet the Superintendent of Police of that area. She refused to go. Kamte Sir then called up the SP himself and requested him to take care of her problem. He was always mobbed wherever he went. Even when his official car passed by, people would stop in their tracks and wish him with folded hands. For school children he was an icon. During the scholarship exam for classes IV and VII, in response to a question asking children to name their favourite leader, a majority of them wrote "Police Commissioner Ashok Kamte."

Col. Sanjay, a friend

"Solapur ka Don, Ashok Kamte aur kaun?" (the hero of Solapur is Ashok Kamte, who else?). This is the slogan that reverberated through Solapur after Ashok had proved his mettle during the riots. In the aftermath of his having handled the situation so well, he earned the nickname 'Don'. And this is how I referred to him in the days that followed—days that turned him from a brother-in-arms to a blood brother.

I must recount here how we met the first time. Solapur being a non-army station had few defence service officers and I had heard that the new Police Commissioner was with an armed forces background. I gave him a courtesy call and imagined him to be an 'old archetype pot-bellied police guy'. When I accepted his invitation for tea and reached his office, I was amazed to see a handsome dashing officer. The tea session spilled over to dinner, as we discussed in detail our favourite topic: weapons. As forced bachelors at Solapur, with his wife and mine in Pune, we spent almost every evening that followed together.

Even though he was an introvert at first, especially when introduced to his civilian counterparts, he made lasting friends during his stay at Solapur.

Our evenings together meant sharing meals. And Ashok, being a typical foodie, loved his meals. Most of the time during meals we would be fighting for the 'few prawns in the curry', and I got a fair share of prawns only when Veenu was around.

Ashok's way of functioning was very military-oriented. He once confided in me that he would be happy to see his elder son Rahul join the army. He took pride in his uniform and the job that entailed being a police officer. He was a stickler for orders and monitored everything happening in his region. His prized possessions were his collection of books on war and on fitness, medals, uniforms and souvenirs from his travels abroad. He was very fond of his weapons too and we often practised firing our air guns at cans during the scorching Sunday afternoons. Even though I am a trained soldier, he beat me on a number of occasions.

He was a fanatic for physical fitness and had a fitness regime that he followed strictly. Both of us worked out together and he was a tough one who could lift 130 kg while I could manage only 90 kg. He was also a great sportsman and played all the games really well. We once challenged each other to a game of squash and at the end of three games both of us were holding our knees in pain. Realising it was too strenuous a game at 40-plus, we moved on to tennis, with no relief! Finally we promised each other never to play such games ever again and gently reconciled ourselves to the fact that working out in the gym was the only safe option left.

For a person so tough on the exterior, he had a soft heart which melted easily enough for those he loved and cared for. What was amazing was to see him get emotional at farewells.

Ashok left Solapur two months before I got my posting, and even though I knew a lot of people there, he left a huge void which could not be filled by anyone. For me, my time in Solapur had become synonymous with Don, as there hadn't been a single day when we had not met or caught up on the day's events. The saving grace was that Pune was our common home ground, so we could meet often even though posted at different places.

In fact, before I proceeded on a posting to Bangalore from Solapur in November 2008, I had two days' joining time and so I went to Pune to meet my family. Out of those two days I spent one day, November 22, with Don at his Chembur home ... and that was the last time I met him. I didn't know then that I would see my friend again only on the television, when the horrifying news of his death was beamed on every channel on November 26. His name had been initially erroneously spelt and that had offered a few minutes of relief till it was confirmed otherwise.

For the few seconds that followed I went through a feeling of absolute vacuum. Even today it is difficult to believe that he is no more. My memories of him and of the great times we shared transcend the capabilities of this narration. For me he lives on. I can still hear his laughter. He is present in his combat uniform that I wear, his Ray Ban shades that I use and his glass that still lies on my table.

Aneesha and Sunil Sadarangani, Industrialists

We were lucky to see the two sides of Ashok. Apart from being a tough cop with a no-nonsense attitude, he was a food lover and loved the *'nalli mutton'* that I cooked. We loved his frankness. He used to find our home very relaxing and once came late at night during the riots to take a break. He never talked about his work: the conversation was always about his college days and sometimes he discussed Hollywood movies.

Our son has made a scrapbook of Ashok who is an inspiration to hundreds of children. We have seen how children would flock to him when he visited schools— it was unbelievable. When he passed away, the entire city was filled with posters and hoardings of him. We had never seen such overwhelming collective grief before. Everything came to a grinding halt and the mourning period stretched for several days. Even now, the city has not come to terms with the fact that he is no more. He used to wear the disposition of the American actor Bruce Willis, with similarity of looks and a shining pate. Ashok also wore his wedding ring the way Bruce did, on the finger of his left hand. The day he was transferred he hugged me (Sunil) tightly and said, "I am going to miss you, man." He was like a miracle that had transformed Solapur.

Yatin Shah, Industrialist

Mr. Ashok Kamte's disposition was very intimidating and it was difficult for anyone to go near him, but somehow I crossed that barrier and we became good friends. We spent a lot of evenings together and I was fortunate to see the other side of Ashok, so warm and hospitable.

He was a man of few words. He loved to have a good spread on his table. When he spent time with us in the evenings, he never talked about his work. He loved his two dogs Hazel and Hillary and I think they helped him relax at the end of the day. He had found a fabulous spouse in Vinita. He would call her up at least four to five times in the evening. He did not have long conversations but would just ring up to say a brief hello, an indication of how deep his affection was.

During his tenure, the *Ganpati* immersion would end right on the scheduled hour of midnight. He once took me for a round on the immersion night—it was 11.45 pm. He laid a bet with me that the procession near the river would be that of the last Ganpati and sure enough it was. We used to call him Don. He took up his *lathi* and brought the city to its knees. He also had a powerful command over his men and they would obey his orders on the double.

∎

CHAPTER 9

THE BEGINNINGS

BHANDARA POSTING

The first time I saw an AK-47 rifle in my life was in Bhandara. It was in 1992, I was newly married and going to set up my home for the first time. It was Ashok's first posting as an IPS Officer.

Only a few years earlier Naxalism had made its advent in the districts around Nagpur—Bhandara, Chandrapur and Gadchiroli. When Ashok was posted to Bhandara, the problem had spread to all the jungle areas of the district. There were very few sophisticated weapons at that time with the police. In fact there were only three AK-47 rifles for the entire district and Ashok had been given one.

Like any young bride, I was looking forward to setting up my new home—warm, loving and secure. The small but cosy cottage housed us comfortably. It was a little isolated and in the evenings we had the company of insects and lizards and at times, particularly during the monsoons, scorpions and snakes. I set about doing up the house. We spent some of the gift money we received for our wedding to buy some new furniture. The cane furniture was covered with some ethnic seat covers, the walls were decorated with some paintings and I managed to make a lampshade out of antlers to adorn one of the walls.

Bhandara was a small town those days and there was little to do. There were no decent theatres, no fancy bazaars and no friends to start with. Ashok was almost always away on operations to the jungle areas and I had little entertainment. Many a times I felt lonely and restricted. My mother-in-law would often call me up from Delhi. She must have sensed my loneliness. On one of our subsequent visits to Delhi, she had a surprise gift for me, a Cocker Spaniel. We named her Cocoa and she was to be my shadow and follow me everywhere.

Satellite television was still new and was available only for a few hours. At times, Ashok used to be away for days at a stretch on anti-Naxal operations and sitting alone at home a sense of anxiety used to pervade me each day till he returned. There was no communication. Those were not the times of mobile phones. My only solace was the *Gayatri Mantra* and the thought of Ashok's courage, which I was sure, would see him through any situation. But once Ashok came back, the house would instantly come alive. It felt as if he was never away. He had the kind of warmth which could pervade the house.

There were arms, ammunition and grenades in the house. Ashok used to explain them to me. From childhood, I always had a fascination for rifle shooting and even attended a fortnight's course at Nasik's Bhonsala Military School. With this background, I was not totally out of place. Occasionally, the officers' wives would visit the firing range and we would try our hand at firing small arms or the .22 rifle.

By now I had grown fond of the cosy ASP's house but it had its own 'peculiar' problems. The house was infested with lizards. I had to literally dodge them whenever I passed from one room to another. In their slimy and shifty way they moved on the curtains, floors, ceilings, walls. Those reptiles with their flickering tongues used to send shudders down my spine. Strangely enough, they would all disappear behind the false ceiling of the roof as soon as Ashok stepped into the house. Whenever I complained to Ashok about the lizards, he would say "Where are they? How is it that I can't spot a single one?" It seemed that they instinctively feared the presence of Ashok. One day, however, I got thoroughly fed up of this menace. Displaying a rare burst of temper I gave an ultimatum to Ashok: "If you don't kill these lizards, I am walking out of the house." Ashok was accurate with the air rifle and the problem was sorted out within weeks.

Though Bhandara was a dusty little town, verdant and thick jungles were just a few kilometres away. Beautiful but dangerous. The Nagzira and the Navegaon Bandh tiger reserves were well within our reach and at times we did visit them. But the scare of a mine blast or a Naxal attack was always at the back of my mind and the visit therefore, was not wholly enjoyable for me. I did not want to say this out of fear of creating concern in others, but Ashok was always unaffected by the risks.

I had known that Ashok had already acclimatised himself to the difficult terrain of the district as well as to the risky nature of the police functioning there. Just a month before I joined him in March, 1992 he had been involved in a major anti-Naxal operation. Two scientists of ISRO had been kidnapped by the Naxalites and the then Superintendent of Police had involved Ashok in a major way in the rescue operations. He had played a key part. The then Superintendent of Police, Mr. Kangale was quick to acknowledge Ashok's contribution in his appreciation letter.

In Bhandara we had to make our own small social circle. We were fortunate to make a very warm and close circle of friends. His first Superintendent of Police, Mr. Kangale and his wife were a warm couple. The next Superintendent of Police, Mr. Aranha and his vivacious wife Mrs. Mariette were more than just our friends, they were our guides and even foster parents. Then there was Col. Jaiswal (Retd.) and his graceful wife. He worked for the local Sunflag Iron and Steel Co. as a General Manager. Frequently, the Nagpur Range DIG, Mr. Rahul Gopal visited Bhandara along with his wife Shangrila. He was a father figure and presided over our small social functions with as much ease as he would direct the anti-Naxal operations with firmness.

When Ashok went for work, I spent my time learning to cook. Ashok was a die-hard foodie, a typical Kamte trait that he carried forward. His grandfather, Shri Narayanrao Marutirao Kamte, had served in the elite police force of the British from 1923. He was appointed as Bombay State's first Inspector General in Independent India and retired in 1955. Shri Narayanrao was well-known in Mumbai and Pune's social circles for hosting exotic, five or seven course meals. The dinners, my father-in-law would tell me, were like formal banquets where guests came dressed in suits and ties. My father-in-law, as a young boy, also had to adhere to this dress code.

Given this tradition, I would often call up my mother to badger her for recipes. Before marriage all I had known was how to cook one or two dishes. One day I told Ashok I wanted to start making baked dishes which would require an oven. We had to get one from Pune. After all the teething problems, we were beginning to settle into a pleasant routine.

Despite all this, I always felt an undercurrent of anxiety in Bhandara. Phrases and words like encounters, mine blasts, ambushes, firing, dominated the conversation amongst the officers at dinners and gatherings. Under these circumstances, whenever Ashok was away, my anxiety at times heightened to panic levels. I recollect one particular evening distinctly.

That morning, before setting out for work, Ashok had asked me to make some baked dish for lunch. The lunch hour arrived but Ashok did not come. I could understand. Ashok was holding charge as the Superintendent of Police, since Mr. Aranha was away on leave. Naturally he was busier than usual. I must have dozed off. When I woke up it was three in the afternoon and Ashok had not yet come. I called the guard outside to find out. I had a sinking feeling when I heard what he said. Ashok had gone to the spot of an encounter in which one constable had been killed and some injured. The encounter was still going on. I did not know who to talk to. The SP was on leave. I spoke to the DIG, Mr. Gopal at Nagpur on phone, he sensed my tension and distress as my voice broke. I was expecting my first child then.

He reassured me that he had spoken to Ashok who was now in the operation and that he was safe and everything was under control. Mr. Gopal also said he would drop in to speak to me. I did not expect him to do that, since the operation was still going on and I had expected him to go to the spot straight away.

However even in that emergency, Mr. Gopal found time to drop in at our home for a few minutes on his way. The gentle and fatherly figure that he was, his visit had a very comforting effect on me. That was to be the first instance in which he was a pillar of support to us. Many followed. He became such an important influence on our lives that we named our first son Rahul, after him.

Another major incident which shook me was the encounter Ashok had on May 3, 1993. It was for this action that the Superintendent of Police, Mr. Aranha, had sent a citation for the gallantry medal for Ashok.

The information was that a Naxalite meeting was to take place some where in the jungles of Magardoh in the Deori Police Station limits. After finding out the location of the meeting through his sources, Ashok reached the spot in the thick of the night with two police parties. After sending one police party a little ahead to take on Naxals who may flee, Ashok reached the spot with the actual ambush party.

As he waited, he saw a torch flashing at a distance of about 40 yards. He flashed back from his own torch. But there was no response. Ashok instructed his men that they would launch the attack and he would fire at the Naxalite who had flashed the torch and that his men should fire at the flanks. The jungles resounded with automatic and other rifle fire. When Ashok had fired his first burst, there was a cry of pain from the other side. Under fire Ashok had advanced. His aim had been to capture the injured Naxalite or recover his body, in case he was dead. But the heavy fire from the other side made it impossible to proceed further. The entire encounter lasted just 15 minutes.

Naxalite literature later recovered had recounted the encounter with the admission that one of them had been injured. Later, Ravindra Sengaonkar, at that time a Dy. SP in the neighbouring Gadchiroli district had independently come across other Naxal literature, wherein they had mentioned a list of people who were to be eliminated. Ashok had figured prominently in the hit list.

So, when Ashok's promotion came in November 1994 and he was posted out of Bhandara as the Superintendent of Police, Satara, it was relief that I had experienced first, rather than pleasure at his promotion. Despite all the tribulations, our Bhandara stay had ended well.

Remembrances
Francis Aranha, the then Superintendent of Police, Bhandara

Ashok was always full of fun. We somehow found in each other kindred spirits. We laughed at the same jokes and could almost know what the other was thinking. I believe I have only enjoyed this kind of rapport with my younger brother who was like a twin to me. I still remember the first time Ashok came home. He was, as always, dressed smartly in uniform with a beret stuck jauntily on his head. He was one of the few people I know who could wear a beret well. Ashok saluted and after a few pleasantries, we began to chat like old friends. I was immediately put at ease by his open boyish charm, his shared love of weapons and his disarming candour in admitting to me that he knew little about computers that I was so fond of.

We got down to discussing the Naxal problem that plagued the district and I soon realised that I had the right person in Ashok to do what I had intended to do— go all out after the Naxals. He had the will, the enthusiasm, and the necessary skills. After all, he had excelled in the outdoor events at the National Police Academy. Barring that first visit to my bungalow, Ashok never entered through the front door again. He would always come the back way through the kitchen, checking with my wife Mariette whether there was anything to eat. Knowing him by now, she would always keep aside something special for him. His favourite was her biscuit log cake.

Despite his professional demeanour, Ashok was like a little boy at heart. He never hesitated to ask for something if he wanted it. I recall we were on camp at a small guesthouse deep in the jungles of Deori Police Station limits, when we were joined by the Range DIG, Mr. Rahul Gopal. Mr. Gopal was wearing a lovely army green jacket which could be switched over to *khaki* on the other side. With big pockets and epaulettes, it looked great. After admiring it, Ashok immediately asked the boss whether he could have it. Mr. Gopal showed no hesitation in saying yes but added that he would give it later since he had nothing to wear at that time to face the chilly weather. Sure enough, he kept his promise, and the next time he was in the area, he delivered the jacket to him, neatly wrapped in a packet.

We spent a lot of time in the jungles—office work in a Naxal-affected area was kept to a minimum in my time, as we wanted to get deep into the problem and deal with it. I had managed to collect data about the Raoji Tulavi *Dalam* and while tracking it, I realised that the *Dalam* was making appearances in different parts of the district at the same time. Unless they could translocate, that was impossible. It soon struck me that nobody actually knew what these people looked like. The real breakthrough came when one of my men in Arjuni Moregaon Police Station picked up a prize catch. It was Ashok who interrogated the prisoner and managed to break into the Tech Apparatus (the intelligence network) of the *Dalams*.

We realised that there were actually village level squads who, by day, were ordinary folk, and by night, went into the jungle to dumps, dug up their equipment and went about committing crimes. They then quietly divested themselves of these clothes and reburied them, becoming 'helpless' villagers once again. By breaking this conspiracy of silence we were able to list and locate all the *Gram Raksha Dalams* which were operating in Bhandara. To Ashok must go a sizeable chunk of the credit for this mission. Acting on information so gathered, we were now in a position to take the war to the enemy. So far, the police had only ventured into the forest in platoon strength or more, with a convoy of vehicles and a lot of fanfare. Not surprisingly, they had never caught anyone.

With Ashok's help, I put together the first group of men who could undertake long range patrol (LRP). Training these men ourselves, we made specialised webbing and clothing for them, drawing on the experience of the Greyhounds in Andhra Pradesh. These 4-5 man teams now fanned out into the jungle, gone for as many as seven days at a time. They had strict instructions to avoid all human habitation, carry their own food and live off the land. They were given detailed maps which I had procured from the GSI and marked with the *Dalam* routes. These were no more than *pug-dandis* (foot trails), but this was where the action was. Ashok, never short on courage, personally led one of the teams. He led the LRP into the jungles, confident that the *Dalam* had been tracked correctly. Vinita was at home with me and Mariette when the wireless began to crackle. There had been an encounter in the jungle, but there was no news of our team. Vinita was distraught. Mr. Gopal and his wife rushed down from Nagpur and we all waited together for news from the party I had dispatched to find these people. It was in the wee hours that news of their safety finally trickled in.

The LRP had come upon a *Dalam* in the jungle and in pitch blackness had traded fire. Ashok, fearless as always, was standing in the face of bullets and returning fire. He was confident he had hit at least one, firing at muzzle flashes. That was the only time in my life I wrote a citation for bravery for the Police Medal. Unfortunately, it got buried in the paperwork somewhere in Mumbai and he never got that medal. The only time I saw Ashok overtly emotional was when I was posted out of the district. The farewell function was organised at the Police Headquarters at Bhandara. All the officers and men were gathered. When Ashok went up to the mike and started to speak, he choked with emotion. We were all pretty emotional, but what really shook me was seeing this man whom I had come to love as a friend and brother, putting his heart out there for all to see.

Mr. Padmanabhan, then trainee ASP Bhandara, now Additional Commissioner of Police, South Region, Mumbai.

In the 70s and 80s, Maharashtra's claim to notoriety was the fact that Mumbai was the haven for smugglers and the underworld, the kind of black fancy, which spawned a genre of badland movies in the eighties and nineties, captivating the imagination of millions across the country.

But what was not known to them and not known even to people in the rest of Maharashtra, was that more than a 1,000 km away from Mumbai, in the remote jungles of Bhandara and Gadchiroli districts, a far more sinister battle was going on, the players unseen, their acts unknown and the heroes unsung.

It was here, in this area, that Ashok Kamte was posted as a young ASP in the sub-division of Bhandara. At that time the district was undivided, and included the areas under the current district of Gondia. The then Superintendent of Police of the District, Mr. Francis Aranha, was quick to assess the potential in Ashok Kamte. Given his penchant for arms, jungle warfare and tactics and considering his supreme fitness, it was only natural that almost from the word go, Kamte was in the thick of anti-Naxal action. He found a perfect foil in the SP Mr. Aranha and the Nagpur range DIG Mr. Rahul Gopal. It was a rare team, whose enthusiasm and fervour was to break the Naxal backbone in the area for over a decade, before they could recoup.

A number of sub-inspectors and inspectors and the constables, who served in that period, under Kamte or who were associated with him in various anti-naxal operations, still recall the gruelling adventures in the burning summers, pouring monsoons and the cold winters.

I as a young trainee ASP was to join the District a few months later in late '92 and was fortunate to be involved with several operations along with Ashok Kamte. Even in those early days, Kamte had become something of a cult figure not only amongst the general public, but also amongst the other officers who followed him into the IPS in subsequent batches. His reputation in the National Police Academy, on his feats in outdoor activities, his level of supreme fitness as well as sheer strength (his shot-putt record is yet to be broken in the NPA), his penchant for action, dare devil attitude and an inborn lack of fear moulded his image that led to adulation even then.

Bhandara in those days was a highly underdeveloped and a small town. The interior jungles did not have metalled roads, the weather was hostile and so was the terrain. Very beautiful to the sight, but very dangerous to tread because of the constant movement of highly motivated Naxal *dalams.*

The police were also ill equipped. The entire district had only three AK-47 rifles, the rest of the men carrying mostly the outdated .303 rifles and a few men carrying SLR rifles. Each foray into the jungle would mean driving on mud roads to the interior and then trekking and tracking Naxals. By the time one reached the spot from where the trek would begin, one would be totally covered in inches of dust. And after this the trek, even in the height of summer where the temperatures would at times try to test the 50 degree mark, on an average Kamte would have done at least about 150 operations in each year of his tenure and each trek would involve a minimum of 25 km in hilly jungles with not even a foot track.

It was under these circumstances, that Kamte was exposed to various facets of a classic anti—guerrilla

operation. There were several instances where he was
fired upon and others where he had to open fire. By
night, by day. He had been ambushed and at times he
had set up ambushes. He had escaped mine blasts and
also beat the Naxal plans by trekking through difficult
tracks to reach a mine blast site instead of using the
vehicle as anticipated by Naxals waiting to ambush.

Days after I had joined the district, I was told to
accompany Kamte as an understudy, on an anti-Naxal
operation. It was my first foray into the jungles on an
operation. Holding a 9 mm carbine, excitement seething
and seated behind, I did not know what was in store for
me. After about an hour into the jungles, where at a
particular point, we had to slow down due to the bad
condition of the dusty road, the Naxalites struck. There
was dust and there was loud sound of firing and the
crash of breaking glass as some of the bullets hit the
windscreen of the jeep. Later we would learn that it was
an attempted landmine blast of the jeep by the Naxalites,
but due to some snag, the blast did not go off. In those
circumstances, where all one can see is thick cloud of
dust, the phenomenon of panic firing sets in. But I still
recall the way in which Ashok Kamte recovered almost
at once from the shock of the attack to fire back in the
general direction of the attackers, at the same time
ordering his men to fire in an orderly manner rather than
to be shooting at random, leading to a situation where
one might run out of ammunition. That was baptism by
fire, and one could see how a brave and well trained
officer could lead, survive and salvage his team even from

an ambush situation.

When he took over in Bhandara, the police fight against Naxals was in an infant stage. Even militant Naxalism in the area was a new phenomenon at that time and therefore, the reaction of the police force in general, was tardy, at least in the initial stages. Officers who served in the Naxal-affected jungles of Bhandara district recall the surprise night visits Ashok Kamte used to undertake in order to sensitise as well as test the alertness of men in the forward posts. He did these almost three or four times a week driving more than a hundred kilometres in the jungles by night.

Ashok Kamte's love for weapons and shooting was well known. In fact, he was the kind of person who was inclined to the martial way of life, if one can say that. He was the Unarmed Combat Competition champion in the National Police Academy, had a penchant for collecting swords and fire arms and stood out in the firing competitions both in the NPA and in the Maharashtra State Police Games. His shooting skills and proficiency with weapons were of much use in the anti-Naxal operations during his tenure in Bhandara.

This was very evident in an encounter with the Naxalites in the height of the summer of May 1993. It was on the 1st of May that the Naxalite *Dalam* led by one Shivaji Tummiretti was chanced upon by a police patrolling party. Firing started instantly from both the parties. Within the first few minutes one police constable was killed and another grievously injured. As the police party pinned down the Naxalites, Ashok Kamte, at that time holding charge as the Superintendent of Police of the district in the absence of the regular SP, rushed to the spot. The constables and officers still recall the clarity of directions and the clear leadership qualities displayed by Ashok Kamte in those circumstances, when the firing was still on. The quality of his firing response was such that, the Naxalites could not retreat with ease, as was the case usually. The *Dalam* commander, Shivaji Tummiretti, who surrendered a couple of years later, recalled the incident clearly. In the firing, one of the Naxalites was injured and he reported that the quality police response was not of the kind he had seen before. A true assessment from the enemy, and nothing could have been more authentic.

Ashok Kamte liked the hard things of life. Heavy exercises, climbing hills, trekking in the jungles, firearms, swords, unarmed combat, shot putting, soccer, basket ball, etc. In all these, he involved his men and inspired them with his expertise and motivated them by example. But all this belied a soft heart. The men under his charge always likened him to a coconut, i.e., a hard exterior with a soft and sweet core. Nothing epitomised Ashok Kamte more than this metaphor. One could see this in the hard and sometimes merciless actions he took against criminals who perpetrated their acts against innocents, had to face the full brunt of his physical prowess, the kind which struck fear in the criminals. This was to be his reputation in subsequent years, wherever he served as Superintendent of Police or Commissioner in districts like Satara, Thane, Sangli, Kolhapur and Solapur.

Those who are acquainted with jungle warfare and left wing extremism and those who have had a part of their destinies intertwined with Ashok Kamte, swear to the fact that it could have only been in the most unfortunate of circumstances, that he could have met his unfortunate but heroic death. He knew all about warfare, urban and jungle; he had undergone ambushes and encounters; had skirted mine infested paths and traps. It was an ambush in an entirely different context that fate had planned for him that cut short a promising and brilliant career.

■

CHAPTER 10

WHEN WE MET

When we bid adieu to Bhandara, Rahul was one month old and Ashok had seen enough challenges to take up higher responsibilities. As for me, the stay at Bhandara helped me see the tougher side of the gentlemanly and suave Ashok who had penned at least two letters a week and called me up every other day during our courtship of eight months. Coming from an elite and cosmopolitan background, his ability to connect with the people at grass root level enamoured me. He treated his constables with respect. He often chatted with them like friends and would ask them about their well-being and their families. I used to always tease him about the anglicised way in which he spoke Marathi but that didn't deter him from conversing in it and that too with great élan.

I was pursuing my post-graduation in labour law in Pune when Ashok came into my life in 1991. My father, Vijayrao Mohite, a well-known criminal lawyer, was very keen that we three sisters pursue the same profession and so we all graduated in law. He encouraged us to be independent. My mother, Jayashree too had done her graduation in law and was visiting faculty in a city college. Thanks to both of them, we grew up as free-thinking women who would not shy away from taking our own decisions. My twin Revati is an advocate in the Bombay High Court and my elder sister Vandana is an environmentalist-politician and the former mayor of Pune.

Along with my post-graduation, it was time for me to 'see' boys to get married. My mother began looking out for eligible bachelors. In a lot of Indian families, the girl's side is always considered as secondary and I didn't want that status for my parents. I wanted that they should also be well-respected. Considering my rather obstinate take on the issue, my mother began worrying that I would remain single. My twin sister was already married and that added to my mother's distress.

One day my uncle, Shivajirao Baraokar, former Director General of Police, Maharashtra, who is distantly related to the Kamtes mentioned to my mother about a bright young man who had just entered the IPS. We were very familiar with the government service cadre. My paternal grandfather, Abbasaheb Mohite, was Municipal Commissioner in the then Baroda State during the Sayajirao Maharaj Regime. My maternal grandfather, Govindrao Salvi was a distinguished District and Sessions Judge during the British era. Three of my maternal uncles, R. G. Salvi, P. G. Salvi and S. P. Mohite were IAS officers, who held several important posts in the Maharashtra

Government as well as at the Centre.

Feeling at ease with the similar family backgrounds, my mother contacted Ashok's father who resided in Pune. "We are interested in your son as a match for our daughter. When can we come and see you?" she asked him. Mr. Kamte, to her pleasant surprise, replied, "We will come and see you at home. I don't stand on these formalities of the girls' side coming to the boys' house." When I heard that, I was quite taken aback. It was such an unconventional response.

My mother invited them for dinner. Impressed by their modern outlook, I looked forward to their visit. My mother asked me to wear a saree and though I kept cribbing, she would have none of my lamentations. Col. Marutirao Kamte came along with his wife and Ashok. I took a quick glance at Ashok. My first thought was that he resembled a Westerner.

He was exceptionally handsome and well-built and seemed reserved. He was probably as awkward or conscious of this formal meeting, as I was. I was amused when his father said, "I call Ashok Tiger and he calls me General." I couldn't help smiling and wondered how a father-son relationship could be so cool and casual. Before leaving, his father said that Ashok and I should meet separately to know each other better.

Ashok called up the next day and invited me for coffee. We drove down to Hotel Blue Diamond where we settled in the coffee shop. Much later I came to know that Ashok's father had instructed him to propose marriage during the first meeting itself if he had made up his mind. He broke the ice by telling me about his life as a police officer. "It is hard for us. We get posted from one place to another. We often live in small towns and work odd hours. We are called on duty any time of the day or night. We rarely have the luxury of a city life," he said.

He wanted to say something more but the waiter kept hovering around us. Ashok kept looking at him from the corner of his eyes, wishing he would leave us alone. The moment the waiter turned his back, Ashok hurriedly asked me, "Will you get married?" I nonchalantly replied, "Is that a general question? If so, yes, at some point of time I will." He smiled and took it further, "Will you get married to me?" I instantly smiled and nodded. That immediately broke the ice and I suddenly seemed to feel a sense of belonging towards him. He too opened up and began telling me about his family.

"My parents are divorced and my father has re-married. My mother lives in Delhi. She is a Sikh and her mother British." That explained his rather unusually fair complexion, I said to myself. Talking more about life in the police force, he said, "You won't be able to lead a free life as you do in Pune. Is that fine with you?" I answered in the affirmative. The three hours rushed by quickly as he described in detail how he conducted raids and chased criminals. He had a very stern boss in Surendra Kumar, he said, from whom he was learning the ropes of being a tough police officer. He dropped me home and I immediately gave the good news to my parents.

On reaching home, Ashok told his father and then

called up his mother in Delhi and informed her about his decision to get married. She, as Ashok confided in me later, was quite taken aback and her first reaction was: "How can you meet a girl just once and that too for an hour and decide that you are getting married to her?" Ashok's reply was, "She fits into our family." His mother wasn't convinced. "How can you make that out in a flat hour?" she asked. "She seems to be a very level headed person. She has made an impression on me. Besides, she has high cheek bones and expressive eyes. That's enough for me." That was the Ashok I was to know—a person who could take split-second decisions with a firm mind.

We got engaged soon after on the lawns of my uncle's bungalow in Pune. Initial apprehensions of being a police officer's wife-to-be were soon erased, with the warmth and affection that Ashok exuded. He would call me every other day. He would write letters to me at least twice a week. He was slowly growing on me. I used to wonder how anyone could be so dedicated as to write letters with such unfailing regularity. I was the one who was lazy to reply, but that did not stop him from writing during our eight month courtship. The tough cop had a soft heart— this trait continued into our marriage and not a single Valentine's Day or Birthday went by when Ashok did not send me cards and flowers.

One day he came to the State Reserve Police Force (SRPF) headquarters in Pune for some training. I excitedly drove there to pick him up after he was finished with the day's work. We spent an evening, chatting and getting to know each other. His sense of humour and witty one-liners used to have me in splits.

During our courtship, he was slated to pass out from the Sardar Vallabhbhai Patel National Police Academy, Hyderabad. I went to attend the Passing Out Parade along with my to-be in-laws. I knew he was an avid sportsman. All that was reflected in the little booklet I held in my hand while watching the Passing Out Parade. It gave the list of the winners in various athletic and field events and Ashok's name as a winner was scripted on practically every event. He had missed the Sword of Honour by a whisker and was a bit disappointed.

He got his first full-fledged posting in Bhandara as Assistant Superintendent of Police (ASP) in Nagpur division and moved there. He told me that the posting was a hotbed of Naxalite activity and that the police had to be constantly on red alert to counter it. One day when Ashok came down to Pune he invited my mother and me to his house in Bhandara. He wanted her to have an idea of where I would be staying after marriage. Ashok put us up in the Sun Flag Guest House as he was friendly with Col. Jaiswal there.

Ashok's house was a charming two-bedroom cottage, impeccably kept. My mother remarked that such neatness was unusual for a bachelor. I noticed, however, that though the furniture was ordinary, the cleanliness and the orderliness gave it a warm touch.

"Now that you have seen what is there in the house, make a list of all the furniture you would require so that we can buy it from Pune," he said to me before we left. My mother was very happy. She was impressed with

Ashok's warmth and hospitality and the way we got along with each other. We got married on February 22, 1992 in Pune. My mother-in-law wanted a typical Punjabi wedding – *'milni'*, *'sangeet'*, *'mehendi'* – all so new to our family tradition. Their entire family had come down from Delhi and Chandigarh.

Ashok refused to sit on the horse. However, after much cajoling from his family members, he agreed to sit astride it but only after the *'baraat'* (procession) had almost reached the corner of our house. We got married in the morning. This was followed by a reception at the Poona Club. After that there was a reception at the Wellingdon Club in Mumbai. I was beginning to know how special Ashok was in every way. He was so caring – ensuring that he always poured tea for me first and ordered all that I liked to eat. He was possessive, affectionate and open-minded—the perfect gentleman and an intellectual. I couldn't have made a better choice.

We began our life together and like Ashok had said, I had to gear up for postings in small towns. I didn't mind it at all. We packed our bags to go to Satara, which was a peaceful posting compared to Bhandara. After the small town, we were going to a big town. The Superintendent of Police's house was a charming British bungalow and I looked forward to staying there.

■

CHAPTER 11

A Chip Of The Old Block

Satara Posting

It was indeed like a breath of fresh air when we left behind treacherous Bhandara for tranquil Satara in 1994. Ashok, when promoted as Superintendent of Police, Satara district, was only 28 years old. I was happy that I was only two hours away from Pune, my parents' home and more importantly, didn't have to worry about Naxalites, jungles and mine blasts. Satara is a pretty town with the Ajinkyatara Fort being the towering citadel that stands guard over this small city, ruled by the Marathas as well as the Mughals at different times in history. Given its chequered background, the district has pockets where Hindus and Muslims reside in almost equal numbers, this factor at times leading to communal differences.

We moved to the official bungalow of the Superintendent of Police, located a little away from the heart of the city. The famous Satara Sainik School, one of the earliest military schools of India sprawled over 150 acres, was right behind this bungalow. The beautiful house had lush green lawns in the front. We had a spacious living and dining area with ceilings more than 30 feet high.

Ashok appreciated my penchant of doing up the house and turning it into a cosy home. Being an interior designer, designing antique styled furniture, Ashok's mother kept an elegant home. We couldn't afford fanciful additions. Nevertheless, spinning art from locally available and affordable material was indeed a delight and a challenge.

The pleasant climate of Satara was very endearing. Its proximity to the hill station of Mahabaleshwar, keeps Satara cool for most part of the year. Every fortnight I would drive down to Pune. We were in the third year of our marriage, and I soon realised that there was no such thing as a 'peaceful posting' for Ashok nor were there any specific office timings that he could adhere to. He was a police officer 24x7, no matter where he was.

For the first time I discovered that duty for him was not only above self but also above any pressure from politicians.

One morning there was a call from the Minister of State for Home, just a few days before the elections. My father and I, who were sitting in the same room, gathered that the Minister was asking Ashok to transfer an Inspector in Satara to a certain place. We were shocked when Ashok replied that he was sorry but could not follow his orders. The Minister was obviously taken aback at this unexpected defiance and blurted out, "Do you know who I am?" Ashok replied, "Sir, I am also the Superintendent of Police."

The Minister whose ego was hurt retorted, "You have insulted me. I will get you transferred." Ashok too responded in an equally fiery tone, "You can get me transferred if you want, Sir." The phones were banged down on both sides. My father and I looked at each other in disbelief. However, I was proud to see the degree of Ashok's uprightness and forth-rightness—it sure needed guts, I thought. The Minister took up the matter with the then Director General of Police, Maharashtra. The DGP called up Ashok to find out what exactly had transpired. When he heard Ashok's side of the story, he called back the Minister and told him that he needed to speak to officers with respect.

Ashok's highlight of his Satara tenure was saving the Maharashtra Police from a major embarrassment. Escorted by the Thane police, five Khalistani terrorists who were lodged at the Thane Central Jail were being moved to the Kalamba Jail in Kolhapur. Ashok received a call stating that the terrorists had escaped from Umbraj near Karad, where they had halted for lunch at a *dhaba*. Ashok was required to apprehend them. He immediately swung into action and formed a special team, which, within 24 hours, nabbed the two who were heading towards Dharwad in Karnataka.

The then Director General and IG of Police, Mr. S. M. Pathania, in his letter of appreciation dated March 29, 1996 stated: "I am writing this letter to bring on record my deep appreciation for the excellent work done by you and your men in apprehending two of the five terrorists who escaped from police custody near Karad on the intervening night of December 3 and 4, 1995 while they were being escorted from Thane Central Prison to the Kolhapur Central Prison. But for your quick response and meticulous planning of the operation, the two terrorists who escaped towards Dharwad district (Karnataka State) would not have been nabbed. The escape of the terrorists from police custody was a serious blow to the reputation of the Maharashtra Police, but I am glad to say that, because of your prompt action, the State Police was able to salvage its name."

My first experience with Ashok tackling lawlessness was when he took us to Mahabaleshwar for a holiday. We were driving down the road besides the Venna Lake one evening. Ashok spotted a physical brawl between the oarsmen of the boating fraternity of the lake and some young boys sporting a crew cut hairstyle. He asked the driver to immediately stop the car and ran down towards the lake. We watched in horror since the oars of the boats were being used as weapons to assault each other. The youngsters were YOs (Young Officers) from the Armed Corps of Ahmednagar, who had come for a holiday. The star attraction for tourists at Venna Lake is boating. A heated argument was going on between the boatmen and the YOs for some reason. This had led to the violent confrontation with both sides having suffered serious injuries.

Ashok went to the spot and moved the two groups away from each other. He waited until both the parties had cooled down. Since the youngsters hailed from a premier army institute, he did not want them to suffer the complications of a police case. I was relieved that he could skillfully settle the matter, for the passions had run so high that the violent argument could have easily led to a fatality or two. He came back to the car and instantly switched roles, back to being a family man enjoying the holiday mood.

Satara, Wai, Phaltan and Karad came under Ashok's jurisdiction. He brought peace in the communally sensitive town of Karad. About a fortnight after he took over as Superintendent of Police, communal riots broke out in Karad on the occasion of the *Holi* festival. Ashok rushed there and quelled any further trouble within hours, much to the surprise of the locals who were used to long periods of unrest. The action was very effective but very unconventional. By day, the residences of the miscreants were identified, but since by day they would be away, they were picked up at night. They were brought to the police station. A tough police constable was deployed for this purpose. Ashok solved the problem in an ingenious way. Seldom had local leaders seen such display of authority before. Determined to make the peace last, Ashok focussed on the town for three to four months after the incident by arresting trouble makers and forming special squads to tackle lawlessness.

Realising that their SP would brook no nonsense, the miscreants fled from there. Peace was restored for many years thereafter.

Sanjay Patil, a well known wrestler and a former member of the Panchayat Samiti was notorious for running illegal gambling dens in Satara. He was in politics and in the past had held the title of *"Maharashtra Kesari"* (the most prestigious wrestling title of the State). Credientials did not matter to Ashok as he firmly believed that no one was above the law even if he or she had political affiliations. Ashok created a stir in the district when he arrested Patil and ensured he served a jail term of 18 months. This action sent out a clear message to the other nefarious antisocial elements and sent them scurrying for cover. Because of such strong actions Satara was rid of the gambling problem for a long time and people recall this even now.

Sanjay Katkar, a senior local journalist of Satara, reminisces how all the illegal activities were wiped out during Ashok's tenure. His daily evening rounds in his official vehicle used to strike fear in the minds of the criminals. Citizens were so overawed with the vehicle that even if it passed through the town with just the driver, they would look at it with respect.

Interaction with the local sporting fraternity was a part of Ashok's professional life, no matter which posting. Once, a cluster of youth organisations hosted a weight-lifting championship in Satara for which Ashok was invited as a chief guest. Ashok not only gladly went there, as he would for any sports function, but also donned the outfit. He told the organisers that besides being a chief guest he would like to be a participant too. The organisers were stunned for a moment and couldn't quite take in the import of that request. Ashok then asked his constable to get his shorts and other accessories from the bungalow. Donning them, he went up on stage and lifted 120 kg of weight, much to the surprise and thrill of the audience. He received a thunderous applause not only for his skills but also for displaying true sportsmanship.

As such, time coasted along in Satara but we knew that it wouldn't be too long before another posting order came through. My happiness knew no bounds when we were informed that Ashok was the only police officer from India that year to have been chosen to pursue a course at the Defence Services Staff College of Wellington in Tamil Nadu. DSSC is one of the few institutes of its type in the world where training is imparted to officers of all the three services – Army, Navy and the Air Force, selected officers of Para-military and Civil Services and officers from other countries.

I was doubly excited since Ashok's baton would get a respite for some time at least.

Vineet Agarwal, who is presently posted as SP, CBI recalls his fond memories of Karad. Source: *The Times of India:*

I still recall the firmness in the handshake I had with SP, Satara, a good 12 years ago. My hand, even after two years of rigorous training wilted under the enormous grip of the former national power lifter. "ASP undertraining Vineet Agarwal reporting, Sir." My voice was louder than necessary, a paltry effort to redeem my pride being squashed with my fingers.

The sternness on the SP's face melted with an infectious smile, "My wife's name is Vineeta and so now I better be careful with what I say to you guys." In a moment, he had drawn me with the personal detail. I felt I had virtually become a member of his family. That was Ashok Kamte, a kind man with a pleasant personality and awesome biceps.

During the communal riots in Karad, a *tehsil of* Satara, he himself led the lathi charge. The final tally—zero casualty, 112 fractures, and no complaints. Interestingly, the people of Karad simply loved him thereafter. I distinctly remember, after the public meeting of a home minister, the crowd flocked to catch a glimpse of Ashok Kamte, the man who broke a hundred bones—a following that would turn in any politician green with envy.

Ashok Kamte liked his drinks. "You should switch over to rum!" he would say. "It's a police drink. No hangover!" But he was a strict disciplinarian. He always began his police station inspection with a parade at 6.30 am sharp. He preferred the beret over the peaked cap and taught me the most gracious manner to don one.

He had little patience for people shying away from action under the cover of legal limitations. "We are men of action, not legal sections," he once told us.

Ashok's grandfather, Mr. Narayanrao Marutirao Kamte too was posted in Satara as Superintendent of Police during the summer of 1929. The British were reluctant to post any Indian there during summer, as

Mahabaleshwar came under its jurisdiction. The hill station wore a celebrity status during the hot months of April and May as British officers along with their families migrated here to beat the heat of Mumbai and Pune. Only rich Indian families patronized it, or rather were allowed to patronize it. His grandfather was the first Indian to be given this 'exclusive' posting.

In his book, *From Them to Us,* he has devoted an entire chapter to Satara. Excerpts:

In April 1929, I received an urgent telegram from the Inspector-General directing me to take charge as officiating Superintendent of Police, Satara with immediate effect. Making a trunk call to Poona, I asked the IG's Personal Assistant how many days joining time I could take; the answer was, "No joining time at all; proceed to Satara at once." I therefore packed my car with my most necessary things, asked my wife to complete the packing up and follow me to Satara later, and set off via Poona.

At Poona, I contacted my maternal uncle and asked him to go to Pandharpur and assist my wife with the packing up and then to help her bring our things to Satara. I also paid a call on the IG at his office and casually brought up the matter of joining time. "Sir," I suggested, "Seven days time is always allowed; even head constables get four to five days; but I've not been allowed even one day." In reply to this respectful protest, my superior officer called me an "ungrateful wretch!"

"Sir," I asked, considerably taken aback. "What have I done or said to annoy you so much?" Then he explained that he had been proposing my name to the Government as DSP Satara for the last month and a half, but it was only now that they had agreed to it. "Skipper Rowland," he finished, "is holding charge of both Satara and Poona districts and he must be relieved of Satara immediately."

I could not help asking, "Why was the government so unwilling to post me to Satara just now?" To which the IG replied, "Never mind about their willingness or unwillingness. You just get along to Satara and relieve Rowland at once."

That same day, 9 May 1929, I reached Satara and took charge. And now I understood why the Government had been unwilling to accept my transfer to Satara at this particular time. Their objection had been, not to me personally, but to me as an Indian.

It must be difficult for our citizens today to picture an India in which almost all the top posts, in every department of the administration, were held by Britons, where the British Raj still flourished vigorously and where any man with a "white" skin was accustomed, and even encouraged, to imagine himself innately and automatically superior to any brown-skinned native of the country. (A British friend of mine has related to me how he was once told by a very senior official's wife, "You know Mr. X, this would be such a delightful country if it weren't for Indians.")

A good deal of police bandobast—security, traffic and so on—was called for during the Mahabaleshwar season and hitherto care had been taken to see that only European police officers were placed in charge of it. I was the first Indian to be given the job, and there was every possibility of clashes occurring. And they occurred. Meanwhile, soon after I took charge, my uncle arrived at Satara with a lorry loaded with my furniture and such of my kit as I had not already brought in my car. Just inside the city limits, he halted the lorry opposite a restaurant and went in to take refreshments. This was on a busy thoroughfare, where parking was not allowed. The constable on traffic duty, unaware whose luggage was involved, objected to the lorry's presence. His questioning annoyed my uncle, who refused to answer, pushed the man in uniform and drove to my bungalow. The constable reported the affair at the Headquarter police station and an offence was registered.

When the ownership of the lorry's contents was discovered, the police came to me and apologised, assuring me that no further action would be taken. But to their surprise I refused the offer. "My uncle has committed an offence," I said, "and you must prosecute him." Much put off by my decision, my uncle requested me to drop the case, but without success. On returning to Poona, he persuaded his sister and my mother to write to me and make me change my mind. In reply to her letter I explained my position, "I must not show any partiality or discrimination between one offender and another; however do not worry about Mamaji as it is not a serious case." My uncle was accordingly prosecuted and sentenced to a fine of Rs. 24/- (which I paid from my own pocket). The incident enhanced my prestige among my police force, who now realised that I was a strict officer and would spare no offender, whoever he might be.

CHAPTER 12

UNIFORM:
A FAMILY TRADITION

For Ashok it was idol worship, quite literally! Since he
was a child, the only photograph that adorned his
study table was that of his paternal grandfather,
Narayanrao Marutirao Kamte, the first post-
Independence Inspector General of Police (IG), Bombay
State. His mother Perm would say, "Ashok was actually
close to my father with whom he spent a lot of time, but
despite not spending much time with my father-in-law,
he worshipped him—he loved him immensely."

N. M. Kamte had served in the British Police Force
since 1923 and then went on to become the first IG of
Bombay State after Independence. His autobiographical
memoirs written in a book titled *From Them To Us* showed
him as fiercely proud, intolerant of nonsense (no matter
who it came from), fearless, of exceptional intellectual
and operational ability and keenly conscious of detail.
What made him remarkable was that he held his head
high despite serving the British by not bowing down to

any unreasonable demands of his 'white' colleagues/ bosses which pointed to discrimination.

Coincidentally, N. M. Kamte made his mark as a courageous police officer when he was posted to Solapur as ASP in charge of the Pandharpur sub-division and was hailed for controlling a major riot that broke out in Solapur. Ashok too made a mark in Solapur during his tenure as Police Commissioner for a similar acheivement; quelling a riot in the aftermath of the Khairlanji massacre in 2006. His grandfather had also served as District Superintendent of Police (DSP) Satara, where Ashok served as Superintendent of Police (SP). Ashok seemed almost like his grandfather's reincarnation as he possessed the same tenacious and fearless qualities and served in almost the same regions.

N. M. Kamte joined the Imperial Police in 1923 when he was 23 years of age. Under the then British regime he served as ASP and DSP in all the divisions of the Old Bombay Presidency (except Sindh), as Deputy Comm- issioner in most branches of the Bombay City Police, and as DIG, Northern Range and CID. He was deputed to the Government of India as Deputy Controller- General of Civil Supplies, and undertook study tours to the UK, USA and Europe. After retirement at 55, he made a successful career in business.

Some of the traits Ashok displayed had clearly been inherited from his grandfather—firmness, decisiveness and determination. Like Ashok did, his grandfather had tamed lawlessness in Solapur decades earlier, almost single-handedly, when all

else had fled. An excerpt from the book:

Solapur was the only large city in the Presidency without a military cantonment and the district administration had recently been in the hands of men somewhat lacking in energy and efficiency. In December 1929, the Bombay Government had sent a senior ICS officer of outstanding efficiency to take charge of Solapur district and tone up the administration. This was Mr. H. F. Knight, once described by a forthright Irish Police Superintendent as the 'best district magistrate I ever served with,' who closed his Indian career as Sir Henry Knight by briefly acting as Governor in four different Provinces in succession. But the sands were running out and the coming trouble could no longer be held in check.

On May 6, information reached Solapur of the wholesale chopping down of toddy palms at Hipparga Tank a short way out along the road to Tuljapur. Mr. Knight and his DSP, Mr. H. R. Playfair, at once set out with a small force of armed police. It was not generally known at the time that Mr. Playfair, a demobilised Army Captain, carried a war wound that caused him much pain every now and then. He was scarcely fit for police duties even in a quiet station, and certainly not fit for Solapur in May 1930.

On reaching the spot where the trees were being chopped down, the DM and DSP told the people to stop their unlawful activity and attempted to arrest one or two of the more prominent offenders. This seemed to enrage the crowd, which proceeded to block the road back to Solapur with felled tree trunks and began to pelt the officials with stones. Mr. Knight who was always averse to firing and lathi charges until they became inescapably necessary, now refused to order such strong measures, even though both he and the Superintendent and some of the police personnel also had sustained injuries from the stones. But the Sub Inspector in command of the armed party made his own decision. Alighting from the lorry, he warned the crowd to disperse, failing which he would open fire. On the crowd's refusal to listen, he ordered his men to fire two or three rounds. The mob immediately melted away, taking with them a couple of men who had been wounded. No one had been killed.

The rest of the story I have had to put together from what I subsequently learned. As the mob wended its way back to the city, it passed the Mangalwar Police Chowky, where one Head Constable and one Constable, both in uniform, were on duty. On seeing these two men, the crowd began to jeer them, accusing them of belonging to the 'rascally' police who had just now opened fire and wounded their friends. The policemen were full of spirit and retorted, "What can you do, you cowards? Be off or you will get a hammering." Their words angered the crowd, one or two members of which cried, "You want to see what we can do?" Still defiant, the policemen answered, "Cowards like you can do nothing."

Some men from the crowd now brought two large empty gunny sacks from a nearby shop, seized the policemen, tied them up and stuffed them inside the sacks with only their heads protruding. Unable to move away, the two men, showing more pluck than discretion, still defied their adversaries shouting, "What more can you do, you cowards! You will have to regret this behaviour." At that the crowd yelled, "You want to see what we can do?" and brought two tins of kerosene, the contents of which they poured over the helpless policemen. Even now the latter recklessly dared the crowd to do anything further. This last taunt was too much to swallow. Somebody put a lighted match to the kerosene-soaked sacks and both policemen were burnt to death.

By this time, the mob had got completely out of hand. It proceeded to the nearby Sessions Court and set it on fire, sending up a column of thick, black smoke which could be seen from all over the city. Some three days prior to the above events, I had gone to Pandharpur, the headquarters of my sub-division.

At a latish hour on 6th, as I sat in the PWD Inspection Bungalow, I was told about the riots in Solapur but nothing about the murdered policemen or the burning of the Sessions Court. I doubted the correctness of my information, believing that if any riots had occurred my Superintendent would have informed me, although Solapur was not in my charge. I dined as usual and retired for the night. At 5 am I was woken up to read an urgent telegram from my superior. It stated: 'Situation serious. Come to Solapur immediately.'

I started in my car at once, and as I entered the city limits I saw an astonishing sight opposite the Navi Peth Police Chowky, which is the first chowky one meets on the road coming from Pandharpur. A white-capped Congressman, clad in white, was directing the traffic. "What are you doing here?" I demanded to know. "All your policemen have run away," he replied, "and so we are doing their duty."

Not knowing quite what to make of this situation, I drove on to my own office, where I found a white cap sitting in my chair! When I asked him what the devil he was doing on my chair, he coolly answered, "Sir, all your police have gone away and so I am doing their duty for them." This was too much for me. "Get out of my office," I shouted, "or I will kick you out." With that I grabbed hold of the man and pushed him outside. Going into my Superintendent's office which was next to mine. I found another Congressman sitting in the DSP's chair. I found the treasury being guarded by a white-capped Congressman holding police rifles. In reply to my query he said: "All the police have run away and we are doing their job of guarding the treasury."

This fantastic situation showed me that things had gone seriously wrong. I went to the Collector's bungalow, which was not far off. Mr. Knight was not there, but his butler told me that his *saheb* had gone down to the Railway Station and that all the *sahebs* intended to leave for Poona by a special train because the situation was too serious. On going to my Superintendent's bungalow, I found Mr. Playfair too had gone to the Railway Station. Then I made for my own bungalow which was about one furlong away. There I had a shave, bath and breakfast and drove down to the Railway Station.

Here, I found all the European men of Solapur, non-officials as well as officials, camping in some First Class carriages at the North Siding. All the European women and children had already been sent away to Poona. In one compartment I found my Superintendent lying on his berth in a state of collapse. At my approach he opened his eyes, murmured, "Have you come, Kamte? Thank God!" and relapsed into a stupor from which I could not wake him. In the next compartment I found the collector exhausted but in full command of himself. He narrated all that had happened, including the murder of the two policemen and the burning of the Sessions Court. He said that all the remaining Europeans intended to camp at the Railway Station, under a strong guard of the Auxiliary Force of India (which was recruited exclusively from European and Anglo-Indian employees of the Railways) and he urged me join them there.

"Sir," I told him politely, "I have just come from the city and everything is quiet there. The only thing is that Congressmen have taken over police duties."

"You were a fool to go into the city," said Mr Knight. "We don't have to have a third policeman killed. Things are very serious indeed and we may have to even abandon Solapur and go to Poona."

"There is no need at all, Sir," I insisted, "to leave here and go to Poona. I am sure we could all go back to our bungalows."

"Please yourself" was the reply, "but it's your own responsibility if you get killed." I saluted my District Magistrate, returned to my office, and sent out to round

up all my absent officers and men. Every one of them
returned to duty at my call, except half a dozen who still
remained absent, and whom I later dismissed for
desertion, after holding proceedings against them.

Hectic days followed. The eyes of all India were on
Solapur. Cipher telegrams (whose purport was often
known in the bazaar before they were laboriously
deciphered by me) arrived for the DSP from all quarters
from the Viceroy downwards and all these I acknow-
ledged, answered or acted upon on my superior's behalf.
After seven days, all the Europeans left their carriages at
the railway siding and returned to their bungalows, where
they were amazed to find that nothing had been touched
in their absence. Looking back on the whole affair, one
cannot help being struck by the discipline and orderliness
—apart from the incidents of the two policemen and
the burning of the court—which were displayed by the
population of Solapur. For hours or even days, the city
lay at the mercy of any miscreant, but no advantage was
taken of this. In a sense, perhaps it served as a small-
scale demonstration of how well India would one day
manage her own affairs after the departure of the British
from India.

**Ashok's grandfather won the adulation of people
wherever he was posted, a quality clearly inherited
by Ashok. His grandfather had a particularly
impressive tenure in Dharwar, Karnataka where he
handled the arrest of a prominent freedom fighter**

Mr. M. D. Karmarkar. The following excerpt shows the sensitivity with which he handled the situation:

When I went to the office in the morning, I was informed that Mr. Karmarkar and another leader, Mr. Hukkerikar, had disappeared and could not be arrested. "I can see very well that someone must have given out secret information," I exclaimed in anger. "I am going to get to the bottom of it and take severe action against the officer responsible for that. Do you think I was born yesterday that you can play tricks like that on me?" I shouted.

For some time there was no trace of Mr. Karmarkar, but one day a letter came from him, addressed to his wife in Dharwar and posted from Bombay. In the regular course of censorship duty I opened the letter and read it, but some kindly feeling made me destroy it without taking action. When a second letter arrived a few days later, I decided that I could not afford to remain inactive. I sent one of my officers to Bombay, who took the help of the city police, arrested Mr. Karmarkar one evening as he was strolling on the sands of Chowpatty and brought him back to Dharwar.

News of his arrest and expected return had at once become public and I anticipated trouble. A large crowd was waiting at Dharwar Station to receive their hero. I too was there with a strong force of fifty armed police, even though I knew perfectly well that the crowd would not find the man they waited for. I had already arranged to have him quietly taken off the train at a flag stop some three or four miles before Dharwar, conveyed to our Police Headquarters which were close by and detained there in the utmost secrecy.

When the train steamed in, all the Congress workers searched high and low to find Mr. Karmarkar. Failing to find him anywhere, they approached me and asked where he was. "That's exactly what I want to know myself," I told them. "You can see me waiting for him here, just as you are doing. But he hasn't turned up and now I don't know what to do," I added. The crowd, which had become greatly agitated on failing to find their leader, dispersed after half an hour.

Next day, a large crowd, which included a lot of school children, gathered in front of the Town Police Station, having somehow got it into their heads that Mr. Karmarkar was being held in the lock-up there. People started pelting stones. On being informed of this, I thought it would be advisable for the District Magistrate to accompany me. This officer, however, (a Briton at that time) shrewdly told me to go without him, saying that he was fully confident of my ability to tackle the situation. On the way I tried to get hold of the City Magistrate, a man with a stammer who was much given to shouting 'arrest the m-man, d-d-disperse the crowd and open f-fire.' But I failed to find him, being told that he had already left to apprise the DM of the riot.

I then went to the Town Police Station and spoke to the crowd, reminding them that Mahatma Gandhi would never ask them to behave violently and throw stones as they were doing. I asked them to disperse, failing which they would get a beating. They stopped throwing stones but began to shout, "We want Karmarkarji." So I invited four or five of the bigger boys from the crowd to come inside the police station and search the lock-up or any other portion to see whether the man they wanted was there. After making a thorough search, the boys were convinced and informed the crowd accordingly.

"Well, if Karmarkarji is not here," the crowd asked in unison, "where is he?"

"That you will have to find out for yourselves," I told them gently. "But now please go away and do not create any trouble here." To my relief, they dispersed.

The parents of the boys in the crowd and other sympathisers had been so sure that the police would open fire that they had kept trucks ready to remove the injured to the civil hospital, where doctors and nurses were standing by to give the necessary treatment. But my handling of the affair with tact (if I may so claim) and without resort to firing created a very favourable impression about me among the Dharwar public. Even the Congress leaders, who soon came to know me well, conceded that I was not the harsh bureaucratic type of police officer.

The affection with which the public of Dharwar honoured me was exemplified in 1976, more than 30 years after I had left the district. I hope I may be forgiven for recalling the incident here.

I happened to have gone to Puttuparthy to attend some 'miracle' performed by Bhagwan Sathya Sai Baba, and together with a friend of mine I was sitting next to a

TO THE LAST BULLET

gentleman who was a pleader from Dharwar. My friend asked this gentleman whether he remembered 'Mr. Kamte, a police officer.'

"Who in Dharwar does not remember Mr. Kamte?" was the response. "He was a most popular officer, and during the Quit India Movement he never harassed our citizens. Even a child knows his name."

"Is that so?" asked my friend. "Well, you can meet Mr. Kamte again—right here!" The pleader quickly rose to his feet, shook hands with me warmly, and apologised for his failure to recognise me on account of the great change which age had wrought in my appearance. He assured me that the public of Dharwar still cherished my memory as that of an 'ideal' police officer.

One week before Independence, Mr. Kamte was honoured by being appointed as Bombay State's first Inspector General of Police. The following episodes from his book will display the forthrightness and discipline of Ashok's grandfather, which was similar to Ashok's style of functioning.

Mr. Morarji Desai (when the Congress Session was held in Nashik in 1950) asked me to invite Pandit Nehru to dine at the Police Mess. I called on the Prime Minister and said that we should feel honoured if he would visit our Mess and give us the pleasure of his company for dinner. The reply I received: "I have not come here for dinners," was as rude as it was curt. I saluted without a word and departed.

When I reported this to our Home Minister, he said, "No, no! How can the PM not visit your Mess for dinner? Let us both go to him and request him to come."

"Excuse me Sir," I replied. "I am not prepared to go to him."

"What a queer man you are!" exclaimed Mr Desai in surprise. "What is your objection in going along with me?"

"Sir even the British Viceroys used to consider it a great honour to be invited to the Indian Police Mess, but our Prime Minister, instead of excusing himself politely, says No to me most curtly and rudely."

"All right, then. Have you any objection if I go by myself and invite him?"

"None at all, Sir. You are our Home Minister and you can certainly invite him if you wish."

That evening, Mr. Desai called me and said that he and the PM would visit the Training School at about 9 pm on Wednesday night and afterwards dine in the Mess. "When he visits the school at 9 pm," I enquired, "will he then address the Sub-Inspector cadets?"

"Yes, he will," I was told.

"Sir," I objected, "9 pm is the time for Lights Out after which no cadet can move outside or even keep a light burning in his room. So how can the PM expect them to attend his address if it's after 9 o' clock?"

"Kamte, you are too punctilious about your rules and regulations. Can't you relax them even for one day—for the PM's sake?"

"I will do anything for the PM Sir. But discipline is

discipline and when the PM is here, is just the time to enforce discipline instead of relaxing it. That would have a very bad effect on the cadets."

"Our AICC meeting is on Wednesday evening," my Home Minister told me firmly, "and we shall be free about eight to eight thirty pm. We shall come to the Training School at that time."

I had pressed my objections as far as possible and now there was no more to be said. I quietly went back to Deolali where I had been obliged to camp in default of any accommodation at Nashik Road.

At 6 pm on Wednesday evening I received a wireless phone message from Mr. Morarji Desai that he and the Prime Minister had decided to visit the PT School earlier than originally planned and would be starting from Nashik Road at 6.30 pm; he wished me to be present at the school to receive them. I at once told my bearer to get out my uniform, but he replied that my wife— doubtless wanting her husband to look smart and neat— had sent it for being ironed and so it was not available. There was nothing for it but to put on my black *sherwani* and white *chudidar* and rush off to the PTS which is eleven miles from Deolali.

We sat down for dinner with Pandit Nehru on my right and Mr. Desai beyond him. All the officers barring myself, were in uniform of course. At the end of dinner, I rose to propose a toast (in water) to the Prime Minister's health. My speech went as follows: "Mr Prime Minister, Sir, I rise to propose a toast to your health. You are a great speaker, a scholar from Cambridge, and a highly educated gentleman. We police officers are not used to giving lectures but are used to carrying out orders." I then spoke few words in his praise and thanked him for sparing the time to come to the Mess. I wound up my speech by saying, "I was very nervous to speak this evening to propose a toast to your health. I therefore asked a junior officer of mine—something which I usually never do—what I should say. And what he advised me was this: "Sir," he said, "please say that we are very happy when the Prime Minister visits our State, but his movements are so sudden that he is a bit of a nuisance!" At this point I looked left and right and continued, "Sir excuse me—there are no ladies present—but he really meant "a bloody nuisance."

The Prime Minister laughed aloud, enjoying the joke but Mr. Desai was bit frightened lest the PM should get annoyed and scold me and so forth. Happily a photograph was taken at that precise instant, which shows Pandit Nehru laughing and Mr. Desai nervously wondering what on earth would happen.

Seeing that our chief guest did not get up to respond to my toast, we all rapped on the table and shouted, "Prime Minister for a reply, please! Prime Minister for a reply!" Then Pandit Nehru got up and said, "Mr. Inspector General of Police and officers of the Indian Police Mess, I thank you very much for inviting me this evening and giving me a sumptuous dinner." Then he spoke a few appropriate words about our work and responsibilities, and ended with "Gentlemen, I promise you not to be a nuisance or even a bloody nuisance. Thank you!" And he resumed his seat leaving us delighted with his generous sense of humour. When the photographs were put before him for his signature, he signed two copies and asked to give him one for himself.

In 1951 when Pandit Nehru visited Ahmedabad, a huge crowd had assembled and N. M. Kamte instructed the DSP to throw a police cordon around the PM's immediate vicinity. Nehru angrily demanded that the cordon be removed. Mr. Kamte refused. He finally removed it when Morarji Desai ordered him to do so as Home Minister.

After the ceremony was over, the Prime Minister came out of the building and stood facing the huge crowd which had assembled. I had already observed the crowd's eagerness to come as close as possible to their hero and the sight had filled me with misgivings which I could not repress. I had therefore instructed the DSP to throw a police cordon around the PM's immediate vicinity and not to allow anyone to break through. On seeing these precautions, Pandit Nehru desired me to remove the cordon. I took no action which made him angrily repeat his request, adding that he did not like to have the police "coming between him and the people." I then explained my inability to do as he asked, since the matter involved the Prime Minister's safety and security. Hearing me argue with the PM, Mr. Morarji Desai pulled me aside saying, "Stop arguing and remove your men at once."

"Sir," I told him raising my voice, "as IGP I am responsible for the Prime Minister's safety and security; you as Home Minister or Shri Kher as Chief Minister, are not. In the circumstances, I regret I cannot agree to remove my police cordon."

Mr. Desai thought for a brief moment, after which he said, "Very well then. But at least you are subordinate to me as your Home Minister and as Home Minister I order you to take your men away. I will accept full responsibility." I then had the cordon removed and the crowd surged forward, threatening literally to submerge Mr. Nehru in the exuberance of their affection.

In his habitual fashion, the PM charged back at the crowd, punching, slapping, kicking, and shouting furiously at them for their utter lack of discipline. All I could do was to keep close behind him and do whatever was possible to shield him from his adorers. Unknown to me, our Chief Minister and Home Minister themselves took shelter close behind me; and as I wielded my cane baton upon those pressing too closely on Mr. Nehru, it was inevitable that I should occasionally strike them also. (Afterwards, Mr. Kher humorously accused me of having "beaten him up," and showed the marks of my baton on his body.) In the general scrimmage, both Ministers had their shirts torn and lost their caps and chappals—for which, of course I had to offer my apologies.

That evening, Mr. Desai wanted me to call upon Pandit Nehru in his special train that was waiting to convey him to his next stop, and converse with him for a few minutes. As a result of the day's unfortunate incident, I was extremely reluctant to do this, but my Minister insisted, and I had to go. And now our PM showed his true greatness of heart. "Kamte," he said at once, "I'm sorry for making a fool of myself, getting your cordon removed. Will you have a glass of sherry with me?"

At my polite refusal, he went on, "Oh, I forgot, you belong to a Puritan State! But see, I order you to have a drink, this time!" Then I put down a couple of quick sherries and returned to Mr. Desai to report what had happened between Mr. Nehru and me. On learning that his IGP had accepted an alcoholic drink, even though offered by the Prime Minster, our austere Home Minister was "not amused."

The book also mentions Ashok's grandfather's contributions in various areas such as recruiting women officers to the force, setting up battalions of a Special Reserve Police, framing new traffic regulations in Bombay, abolishing the Silent Zone and introducing various Welfare schemes, and initiating a system of *taktas* or Information Boards which gave an immediate indication of the current position regarding all serious crime in the State—murder, dacoity, house-breaking and so on.

Ashok's great grandfather Marutirao Kamte
Ashok's great grandfather, Inspector Marutirao Kamte who served the police between 1895 and 1923 died with his boots on. He was presented the Sword of Honour

(which adorns our home even today) by Lord Willingdon, Governor of Bombay Presidency.

N. M. Kamte writes in his book:
Nestling at Purandhar's foot is the little village Chambali, where my great grandfather Laxmanrao Kamte owned and farmed some fifty acres of land, raising good millet and fruit as well as a sturdy crop of sons.

In 1850 one of these sons, Tukaramji, entrusted his small share of the family land to a brother, and betook himself to Poona, where he secured service as a *pattewala* in the office of the Collector, the civil Head of the district. In those days of simple living and low prices, my grandfather's salary of Rs. 18 per month was a tolerable wage. (His son, Marutirao was N. M. Kamte's father).

Marutirao joined the police service in 1895 as *Jemadar*. After serving as Sub-Inspector at various places in Poona District and finally in Poona city, he was promoted as Inspector and spent many years in the Criminal Investigation Department (CID). His meritorious services which included security duties on deputation at the Delhi Durbar of 1911, were recognised by the titles of Rao Saheb and later Rao Bahadur, by the award of the Indian Police Medal and the King's Police Medal and by a Sword of Honour presented to him by Lord Wellingdon, Governor of Bombay Presidency (which then included much more than today's Maharashtra State) in 1913.

N. M. Kamte attributes his father's success to the

following qualities which seemed to have been passed
down the generations:

"My father's success in the CID was due to his
possession in generous measure of the good detective
qualities of hard work, persistence, painstaking enquiry,
imagination and ingenuity, and—where all else fails—
what I would call enlightened ruthlessness."

N.M.Kamte also recounts the adulation, love and
affection bestowed on his father by subordinates,
colleagues , superiors and the general public;   similar to
what Ashok was to receive years later.

Writes N. M. Kamte, "That day was July 3rd, 1923, the
fiftieth anniversary of my father's birth. What a tragic
irony it was that he could not himself convey to us the
joyous news of my selection! However, the funeral which
the State Police gave him and the tributes paid by
hundreds of his friends amply testified to the love and
respect he held. The Inspector-General who sent his
personal assistant Mr. J. B. Jacob to represent him,
directed that the cortege should be escorted by a detail
of armed police with the Police Band to play the Funeral
March. The procession was halted again and again by
merchants and fruit-sellers and other common folk who
had not forgotten his many kindnesses when he served
in Poona City. The bier was profusely garlanded and many
of my father's colleagues came in person to the burning
ghat. After the escort had fired a volley, bugles sounded

the Last Post."

Lt. Col. Marutirao Kamte, Ashok's father

Ashok's father Lt.Col. Marutirao N. Kamte was
commissioned in the year 1950 to the 1st Guards. During
his illustrious career he was the ADC to the Chief of
Army Staff General Rajinder Singhji. Later he was the
Adjutant of the Indian Military Academy, Dehradun. He
was also part of the team sent to set up the Military
Academy in Nigeria. He was also part of the UN Peace
Keeping Force in Vietnam. Amongst other places he has
served in Kashmir and Leh. His father's Armed Forces
background shaped Ashok's love for uniform, weapons,
military history and military band music. It is from his
father that Ashok imbibed the qualities of discipline and
hardwork. On his retirement from the Army, Lt. Col. M.
N. Kamte ran a successful Security Services business with
which he is still occupied.

Dr. H. S. Bawa, Ashok's Maternal Grandfather

Ashok's maternal grandfather Dr. H. S. Bawa was one
of the direct descendants of the Sikh Guru Amar Dasji.

Dr. Bawa has scripted his lineage in the book *Bawa
Budh Singh – A homage* wherein he has biographed the
story of his father, Bawa Budh Singh (Ashok's maternal
great grandfather), who worked in the elite Indian Service
of Engineers (ISE) during British Rule. He was also a
well-known scholar, having written a number of books. ∎

CHAPTER 13

FAIR AND FEARLESS

SANGLI POSTING

Nestled on the banks of the River Krishna, the historic town of Sangli borders Karnataka State. Its twin town Miraj is well reputed for offering advanced medical facilities despite its rather remote location in Western Maharashtra. Thanks to the co-operative movement, Sangli district is a predominant centre for sugar mills, turmeric trade, grapes and other horticulture and processed agro-products.

Sangli on the face of it looked serene and peaceful. It belied the undercurrents of political and social tensions which Ashok was soon to confront. Within a week of taking over as the Superintendent of Police of Sangli district, Ashok was to face his first test. A dreaded criminal Raju Pujari, who had created terror in the district for over a decade had ventured once again into his well known trade – extortion. He had not perceived the change in the scene.

He was killed in an encounter within a week of Ashok

taking over. It took place on one of the arterial roads of Sangli town in the dead of the night of August 30, 2002.

It was for the first time that Sangli District had witnessed a criminal being killed in an encounter. There was delight and the people heaved a sigh of relief.

The problem of extortion came to a head within days of Ashok joining as the SP of the district. On the sixth day of his new posting, in the evening, at about eight, a noted industrialist of the town got an extortion call from Raju Pujari – the most notorious extortionist and *goonda* of the town.

Raju Pujari, originally from the Udipi district of Karnataka started as a tea vendor when he came to Sangli first. A short while later he entered into petty crime and within years he had graduated into big time crime and was now the most feared *goonda* and extortionist of Sangli. He had six murder cases, sixteen extortion cases and innumerable other criminal cases filed against him over the years. He had also been booked under the Maharashtra Control of Organised Crime Act (MCOCA). The moment he came out of prison, which was a week before he was killed, he began his criminal activities with renewed vigour.

An industrialist approached the Vishrambagh Police Station on the night of August 30, 2002, with the report that Raju Pujari had called to make an extortion demand. When the matter was conveyed to the new SP, the complaint was taken with all the seriousness it deserved. In fact, the reaction and response was not the kind ever seen before.

With his earlier experience of dealing with such situations in Mumbai and Thane, Ashok was pretty clear in his directions and organised in his responses. He immediately formed a crack team under the leadership of Dy SP Mr.Vishwas Pandhare. The word was clear, that the gangster should be dealt with firmly. At the same time, Ashok also put on job several seasoned constables to get information on the whereabouts of Raju Pujari.

The industrialist had informed the police that the gangster had said that he would come at about two in the night to his factory, Vijay Industries. Ashok had deployed his teams around the area. Around midnight, he received information that Pujari would be coming from the direction of the 100-foot road towards the factory and he immediately gave appropriate directions to the teams lying in wait to apprehend the gang.

What happened was a little unexpected. But Ashok's directions had been clear—that the strongest possible action should be taken as the situation demanded. Dy. SP Pandhare formed two teams and they had been placed at strategic locations to nab Pujari. As soon as one of the constables spotted a red coloured 'Boxer' motorcycle he alerted the others. Pujari was riding pillion. Pandhare came on to the road and gestured to Pujari, to stop and surrender. In response, Pujari, pulled out his Japanese make revolver from his waist and started firing. In return, Pandhare fired back at Pujari and injured him. Raju Pujari fell injured and the motor cycle rider ran away. The police quickly rushed Raju Pujari to the hospital where he was declared dead on arrival.

The encounter sent shock waves, not just through Sangli, but also in the neighbouring areas. It was the first ever encounter in Sangli city. The incident was all over the newspapers. Coming within a week of the new SP's posting, the encounter sent shivers down the spine of many a criminal. Some of the officers posted in the district at that time recalled later that, hardened criminals fled not only Sangli town, but the district itself.

In the press conference held in the morning, Ashok's message was clear. Criminals will be dealt with an iron hand. This clear message from the SP set the trend— the city as well as the district witnessed a sharp fall in *goonda* related crimes and extortion threats. There was palpable relief in all quarters.

Popularity followed Ashok wherever he went in the district. In public functions, *bandobusts* or private visits, people mobbed Ashok.

As in other places, in Sangli too Ashok kept up his fitness regime. He would go for his regular evening jogs at the police ground every day after work. The grounds would be filled with citizens of all ages. Seniors taking a leisurely stroll, and youngsters playing cricket/basket ball were a common sight. The new feature was the police chief of that town, running in sparkling white shorts, T-shirt and white shoes. Constable Shrikant Kumbhar remembers: "There would be people specially coming to see Kamte Saheb. Several youngsters and children would run behind him. Saheb never felt conscious about this fan following—in fact, he took it in a sporting spirit."

Ashok won the hearts of his constabulary here too.

The day he joined office, the first place he visited was the constables' mess—where the men dined. He wanted to inspect the mess and see the conditions for himself. He was happy with the quality of the food and gave a few suggestions for improvement.

He loved the Police band of Sangli. He would say that it is next best to the Army band. I remember that, so overwhelmed was he with the superior quality of the band and the dedication of the constables, that he gifted the surprised Band Major with a decorative vest which was an ancestral acquisition. Being a music aficionado himself, his ears were trained to hear good music and appreiciate it. He was particularly fond of military band music being an Army Officer's son.

Another incident in Sangli which made Ashok popular with his men, was during the Kolhapur Range Police Games held at Sangli. The Sangli Police team was trailing. But only till their SP entered the court. The tide turned soon and Ashok had 17 baskets to his credit. His team won. People had known only about his shotputting, athletic and weightlifting skills till then. His basket ball skills added to his aura.

Sangli has always been sensitive. Even small incidents raised the passions of the people. Prior to Ashok's tenure when a six year old boy Ritesh Deotale was kidnapped and killed, it was not surprising that the entire town was up in arms. The kidnappers were nabbed by the police within a week, but the town was clearly enraged. The trial which took place during Ashok's tenure was a public affair. Thousands thronged the Court premises during the hearings. Passions had risen and the public was rooting for a death sentence.

Ashok was very intuitive and could gauge the public mind. He was well prepared on the day of the judgment. More than five thousand impassioned people had gathered when the sentence was announced—life imprisonment. The public reacted, but the police was well prepared. For the first time the public saw the sterner side of Ashok—he himself took charge and within minutes the crowd had dispersed. But the diehard ones still waited for the accused to be taken out. There was a distinct possibility of the crowd attacking the vehicle carrying them. When the vehicle came, they were disappointed. It was a dummy. Ashok had moved the accused in another van from the rear of the Court premises, away from the public gaze. Even in those circumstances he had displayed foresight.

Those days the Shetkari Sanghatana was agitating for better prices for sugarcane. The villagers recognised no authority. They would sound a siren whenever any government vehicle approached, and the people would pour out on the streets to oppose. Police vehicles were no exception. On a particular day, in a village called (Mauje) Dighraj the agitators turned violent. They went berserk and there was a lot of damage to both public and private property. When the police tried to intervene the public reacted against them too. Some policemen were injured and the agitators locked up the other policemen in some of the houses. Ashok was on leave at that time.

Back from leave, Ashok was apprised of the situation. Now the police had a more serious case against the agitators—of confining and injuring policemen. Despite the political sensitivity of the issue, Ashok decided to be firm. He sent out teams to arrest the agitators who had indulged in the violence.

This was a different kind of operation for the police, in the sense that they were going to apprehend people who had actually beaten up police on duty. The arrests were not going to be smooth and the agitators resisted. The situation went out of control and there were alleged excesses by the police. Both the sides sustained injuries. The entire incident assumed political overtones.

There was an uproar. There were calls for heads to roll. Normally in such situations, the officers and men would have been let down.

Ashok who had briefed his men and officers before the operation, took full responsibility for what had happened—even though he was not present during the incident. The men and officers still recall how he was a leader in the true sense.

The then Divisional Commissioner of Pune Division had inquired into the incident. He was to remark about Ashok later that rarely had he come across an instance of a senior officer standing up for the actions of his juniors. That was Ashok.

Remembrances
Puranjay Jadeja-The Ashok I knew

Little did I know that one casual visit to his office in Sangli to hand over my company's diary would result in such thick friendship.This was in 2001 when I was posted in Sangli with BPCL.

He came across as a man who loved guns, action, food, dogs and above all who energised everyone who came in touch with him. I can never forget the way he used to greet me in his booming voice by saying "Hi Puranjay" full of life coupled with the most endearing smile that only a child could have. This would be followed by a firm handshake or a bear hug.

Our only dinner guests in Sangli were Ashok and Vinita. Ashok, even without exchanging any greetings with me would go straight to the kitchen to check out what was cooking. He would look at the food, inhale and announce — smells good. Then as the evening progressed there were three songs which we would always play with our drinks, *Knocking on Heavens Door* by Bob Dylan, *Horse With no Name* by America and *Life is a Roller Coaster* by Ronan Keating.

He looked forward to his meal, was generous with his compliments and was totally unapologetic about choosing the best piece of meat from the bowl. Each time our *rotis* swam in our curry, we pledged not to touch red meat but we never got to adhering to it. He was like that—totally accepting his weaknesses for food, as he accepted them in others. He couldn't be bothered to be politically correct. He was someone who called a spade a spade. I think it came from being childlike and innocent in so many ways. He was completely without any malice. Whenever I had a meal with him in Chembur, he'd coax me into giving his cook a handsome tip—the fellow needs to know he's appreciated, he'd say.

I admired his fluency in English. Once in Sangli we were enjoying a barbeque that Vinita had organised, Gayatri, Vinita and Revati challenged him to tell them the meanings of words that they chose from the dictionary. He was so accurate with the meanings of all the words, that we thought we'd have to eat humble pie till he got stuck on the word 'pew.' He later admonished himself playfully for not being able to recollect something he actually knew.

What I loved about Ashok the most was that I could be myself with him with all my faults. Ashok was the only person I was totally comfortable with and at times on Sundays we would be spending long hours, so many of them in silence, just listening to music.

I just cannot forget the awesome mutton pickle that he would serve us in Sangli, and when we went to celebrate the New Year at his house in Pune in 2004, he thoughtfully packed two jars of my favourite pickle.

Our talks would be centered around fitness, weapons, fighting tactics and music. I thought I knew all about guns till I met him.

I still remember vividly the night of Nov 24, 2008. I had just returned from Bangalore after a Golf tourna- ment. Ashok had invited me to have dinner with him, promising a delicious spread. I declined as I had an early morning flight the next day and was tired. Ashok was difficult to refuse and I finally joined him for dinner that night. I would have never pardoned myself if I had not gone that evening. I am unable to come to terms with 26/11. Ashok is and will always be with us forever.

■

CHAPTER 14

THE FOREIGN ASSIGNMENT

BOSNIA POSTING

One of Ashok's batchmates and good friend Mr. Sanjay Kundu, who accompanied him to Bosnia reminisces:

The war in Bosnia had torn the country on ethnic lines. International efforts were launched to provide military, police and civilian assistance to stabilize the country and bring peace back in the Balkan Region. The United Nations-International Police Task Force (UN-IPTF), under the aegis of UN Mission in Bosnia & Herzegovina (UN IBH), was formed with Police Officers from over fifty countries with the mandate to establish 'rule of law' in the war torn country. India was a major contributor to the UN sponsored IPTF, and played a leading role in bringing peace to the Balkan Region.

Ashok Kamte was selected to represent India in the prestigious UN-IPTF during 1999-2000. The selection process was tough, gruelling and extremely competitive.

The UN-SAT team from New York tested over 1,000

Indian Police Officers especially for their skills in policing, English language and driving, but only a few were selected. Ashok was among the top in the list of successful candidates selected for the UN mission and was part of the Advance Team from India to reach Sarajevo in July 1999.

Ashok quickly established himself professionally within the UN system. After his induction training, he was assigned to the prestigious Sarajevo IPTF station. His affable personality, strong leadership skills, excellent professional knowledge was soon recognised by the international community. He was assigned an array of responsible positions: Chief of Operations, Property Officer, Training Officer, Human Rights Officer and Station Commander. Ashok got along excellently with Police Officers of over fifty countries and the local Bosnian staff.

Working in Sarajevo, Ashok endeared himself to all the three ethnic groups, namely Bosnians, Croats and Serbs by setting personal example of fair play and justice. As a key member of the Sarajevo UN management team, Ashok implemented the UN mandate in its true letter and spirit.

The Bosnian tour was very satisfying for Ashok personally. He was one of the few Indian officers who made friends with foreign police officers, and was extremely popular with the international community. His love for travel took him to many places around the world, the opportunity which the UN assignment amply provided him.

A gym buff, Ashok was regular at the Butmir U. S. Army Base gymnasium. His gymming and power lifting skills overshadowed even the Westerners and he won many championships organised by the international community.

Ashok always remembered his Bosnia tenure fondly. He was particularly close to one German Police Officer, Wolfgang. Wolfgang was so influenced by his friend that he named his newly born after Ashok. The flexible person that he was, Ashok did not face any problems with food during his tenure; he always enjoyed continental food. A year later, when he returned to Pune, he was fighting fit, having trimmed down nicely.

In keeping with his passion for music, Ashok brought back with him CDs of Bosnian music and insisted on playing some of that country's famous numbers at home and family parties. None of us knew that Bosnia had such foot-tapping modern folk compositions, peppered with pop music and influenced by Serbian and Turkish tunes. We used to thoroughly enjoy listening to them, while Ashok reminisced about his Bosnia experience. ∎

CHAPTER 15

AVID SPORTSMAN AND FITNESS FREAK

6 pm: Appointment at the gym. This was one rendezvous that remained unchanged, no matter where Ashok was. A dedicated body-builder, his biceps were as awe-inspiring as his baton. As a power-lifter, he had broken three National records and won half a dozen gold and silver medals. His adroitness in 100 metres, 200 metres, shot putt, discus throw and high jump brought him laurels in school, college and police competitions. He was a good cricketer and was a sportsman to the core, backed by physical strength that he honed day after day, relentlessly.

His passion with physique strengthening began as a teenager. Says his mother, "From a lanky school boy to a muscular teenager (when he was in St Stephen's College), the transformation was indeed amazing and quick!" What irked her though was the special evening booster drink that he made for himself. Consisting of two litres of milk mixed with 12 raw eggs and six bananas, this post-gym evening fad had his clothes smelling 'eggy'. His mother protested, saying, "Please don't have this drink in front of me." She said she could not bear to see him guzzle that huge jug of liquid, but that didn't stop Ashok from his pursuit to build his body. He would then have it on the terrace of his house but still his mother complained of the eggy smell that pervaded the house, because he was making it in the kitchen. Not one to be bogged down by this protest either, Ashok then found a willing accomplice in a friend who also religiously consumed this booster drink and both would have it at the friend's home.

The strength of his muscle power is reflected in an incident narrated by his mother. During his graduation days in St. Stephen's College, he used to regularly spend his evening at the Khan Market, a popular shopping arena in Delhi. He used to park his scooter in the space allotted for parking. One evening however, a car driver decided to park at that very spot. He got down from the car, pushed the scooter (it fell) and parked his car in that space. When Ashok came back to where his scooter was, he asked around as to why it had been thrown away in this manner. Outraged at what he was told, he simply moved the Fiat single-handedly and shoved it away. The people around were stunned at this act. Word spread like wildfire and shopkeepers came to witness this drama. "From that day," says his mother, "he became famous there. This took place more than a decade back, but whenever I went, they enquired about him, specially the shop from where he used to buy pork. Nowadays, they simply do *'Namaste'*... they don't know what to say to me."

Since he was four years old, his mother, who herself was a National level squash champion in 1956-57 and represented Delhi for table tennis and badminton, would take them to the Indraprastha Stadium in New Delhi. Says his mother, "Every evening during vacations, since they were little kids, I would take both Ashok and his sister Kiki (Sharmila) to the stadium to hone their sporting skills. While Ashok excelled in shot putt, discus throw and running, Kiki represented Delhi in high jump. Until Ashok made himself heavy to become a weightlifter, he won many accolades as an athlete." Mr. Balachander, Ashok's Physical Education teacher at the Kodaikanal International School though remembers the tinge of frustration Ashok felt as he could never triumph in the long jump event. Says he, "Ashok would try so hard to get that step right for long jump but would never succeed and always missed being the long jump champion."

Ashok was seven years older than Sharmila. As a responsible 'big brother' he would make her run in the Lodhi Gardens in an effort to increase her stamina and strength. Ashok insisted on weight-training for her as she was a lanky girl. Sharmila who is a professional dancer and choreographer attributes her agility and fitness to Ashok, who introduced her to weight training at a young age.

What made Ashok a formidable sportsperson was also his intense capacity to bear physical pain which seemed to be an innate quality. As his mother points out, "When he was a child, he would often fall and hurt himself. Once I remember, he was climbing up the gate of our bungalow and one of its spikes pierced his stomach. I was horrified, as I picked him up from there, but he hardly cried. I was the one always left crying when he got hurt, but injuries just didn't bother him."

It is probably this endurance that made Ashok into a dynamic sportsperson. One of his classmates, Nitin Raikar of Rajkumar College, Rajkot, the prestigious residential school where he studied, recalls a game of hockey with Ashok. This is what he has posted on the alumni website after he heard the news of Ashok's death:

"We were together from 1972 to 1977 and I would like to recall a small incident here which reflects Ashok's dashing personality in his early childhood days. I am sure we all remember Northground and the hockey/football ground just opposite Mr. Lal's (our flamboyant English teacher) quarters. It was here on this very ground that I still vividly recall a small but significant incident which made Ashok into my life size hero instantly.

"We were engrossed in a small game of hockey during our routine games period and both of us were in the same team. He was playing in the Centre Forward position while I was in the Right Position. We had almost succeeded in getting into the 25 yards circle near the goal post and I was in full control of the ball with my adept dribbling. Ashok yelled at the top of his voice commanding me to shoot the ball in the goal and I, with all the feeble strength that I had in those days swung the hockey stick wildly... only to see the stick missing the ball and cracking Ashok's jaw! With blood trickling from his jaws, Ashok gave me an icy stare followed by two tight slaps on my face which shook the daylights out of me! A few minutes later he was back in action, and I was still cowering in fright in anticipation of the off-field repercussions!! Such was the charisma of Ashok—an absolute fighter to the core. With all the childish innocence I offered him my pleading apologies and he was quick to dismiss it as an accident. After half time we were both back in action and Ashok leading our team from the front... to victory!

"I recollected this incident to Ashok when he was posted in Kolhapur as Superintendent of Police and he was totally zapped by my memory recall. Well, it probably is because I was at the receiving end!"

At the Kodaikanal International School where Ashok studied from Std IX to Std XII, he was renowned as a sportsperson and had attained the status of a star. He would always walk with his chest upright and his head held high, says Mr. Balachander and adds, "While other boys of his age went for leisurely walks and to discos in the evening, Ashok would always be found at the gym. He was very proud of his physical strength and would also cajole others into following a fitness regime. He was the undisputed champion in various athletic events and shone brightly at the prestigious annual inter-school sports tournament that was held in Ooty." Mr. Balachander adds that, "It is rare for a school boy to be so dedicated to sports and so focused in life. He always played to win."

A write-up in his college magazine reveals Ashok's reputation as a fiery sportsperson. It states: "The class of '82 was enriched when Ashok, one of the most talented guys of our class, joined us in 1978. One thing we constantly rediscovered about Ashok was his love for sports. He starts and ends all his conversations with sports. One could see him with a shot-putt at 6 am as well as at 6 pm. Never discouraged by anyone or anything —if he broke his leg, he would continue with his hand and vice-versa. He has made many tremble in racquetball courts with his powerful and vicious shots which many are afraid to face. One never sees him taking it easy or giving up in any game from ping pong to soccer."

What fascinated his teachers and school friends was that despite being a sportsperson with a killer instinct, he was always ready to prod others to win and help them to become better sportspersons. The write-up ends with Ashok's warm heart that he was also known for. It states: "This is Ashok as known to many but very few know the real Ashok, the kindness and the loving part of him, which has been discovered by a few. Ashok, we are surely going to miss you and your uniqueness. Farewell, wherever you may go—be it Delhi, Oxford or Olympic grounds."

Sports indeed was Ashok's passion which continued even when he joined the elite police force. In fact, during his one-year tenure at the National Police Academy in Hyderabad, after he was selected in the Indian Police Service (IPS), his batchmates remember him as an outstanding sportsperson with immense physical strength. Dr. Upadhyay, present Police Commissioner of Solapur and his IPS batchmate vividly recalls Ashok as possessing awesome physical strength, being a firebrand sportsperson and a warm-hearted human being.

Dr. Upadhyay fondly recalls, "Ashok and I belonged to the 1989-90 batch of IPS. We were in the same squad during the 18 months of training at the National Police Academy, Hyderabad. He was the most outstanding person because of the charisma he exuded and his expertise in all physical activities. He excelled in all athletic events and was always the centre of attraction. Most IPS officers come from good academic backgrounds and are equipped with a strong intellect. However, their attention to physical development suffers. Ashok was an exception as he trained himself to be always 'fighting fit.'

Recalling an incident which showed Ashok's magnanimity, he says, "I saw his humane side during a cross-country race at the Academy. During such a race, we are allowed to carry a limited quantity of water which is to last us till the end. I was running alongside him and felt thirsty at one point. Ashok had some water left in his bottle. He quickly offered it to me, despite the fact that he had a long way to go. I was touched by his gesture."

Maharashtra's Police Force received an unprecedented impetus in sports competitions due to Ashok's deep involvement in promoting them. When Ashok handled recruitments, constables with sports background always had an edge. He took personal interest to hone their skills at games and motivated them towards enhanced physical fitness.

Constable Jarag, who was his gunman during both his Mumbai postings – in 2000 and 2008 – recalls, "When Kamte Sir was posted as DCP Zone I, in 2000-2002, I was called to his office on the first day of his taking charge as I was appointed his gunman. After he briefed me, I turned to leave, when he noticed my limp. He stopped me and inquired about it. I told him of my accident eight months ago, because of which I still could not walk properly. He asked me to accompany him on his daily walk at the Oval Maidan. For six months thereafter, I walked behind him, while he did many rounds of the *Maidan,* wearing an iron vest weighing 15 kg. The vest used to be so drenched with Kamte Sir's sweat that it used to take 24 hours to dry. Thanks to Sir, my limp completely vanished and I became aware of the importance of physical fitness."

Ashok was a voracious reader of fitness and nutrition magazines and books. He was always aware of the latest updates on this subject. He has an impressive collection of sports and fitness books in his personal library at home. He used this knowledge to ensure that nutritious food was being served in the Constables' Mess, especially when they were training before a big tournament. He enjoyed playing various games with his constables and set up gymnasiums wherever he was posted. He encouraged his men to include workouts as a part of their daily regime because he believed that fitness keeps both mind and body agile, an important requisite for police personnel. He organised sport events for his men and showed his appreciation when they excelled.

Ashok has won innumerable awards for sports since his childhood. The description 'Jack of all trades and master of none' did not hold true for Ashok, as he excelled in every sport that he took up. The exhaustive list of certificates, awards and medals says it all. He played both, individual and team sports: shot putt, javelin throw, tennis, swimming, basketball, hockey, football, weight-lifting. He won the best all-round sportsman prize at St. Xavier's College in 1983-84. He was the Maharashtra champion in shot putt; was National Champion in Power Lifting and won the Maharaj Singh Trophy at the National Police Academy at Hyderabad and the Akruti Cup for unarmed combat.

The following letter written to me by Constable Shrikant Kumbhar speaks volumes of Ashok's commit-ment to encourage sportspersons in the police force and the affection and respect with which he treated his men:

"On January 6, 2003, Ashok Sir recruited me into the police, during the open recruitment scheme in Sangli. He used to choose candidates based on their physical fitness and excellence in sports and I was glad to have met his expectations.

"I joined the police force on January 16, 2003. Before going for my training at the Nagpur Police Training Academy, I was posted for one month at the Sangli Police Headquarters and we had to compulsorily do a certain set of tasks apart from the regular duties. I was assigned to work in Sir's bungalow from 4 pm every day. Kamte

Sir had instructed the drill instructor that I be assigned the simple task of watering the garden. This was told to me by Kamble Dada, a peon working with Sir at the bungalow.

"One evening, as I was watering the garden, Kamte Sir got into his car to leave but then instructed the driver to stop near the gate. I was called for and that scared me a bit. Had I done something wrong? I was literally trembling but was pleasantly surprised when, instead of pulling me up, he gave me some money and said it was a reward. Sir then explained that the driver and he had been discussing about whether I was an athlete or weight-lifter but then finally what mattered was that I was a sportsman. I was so taken aback, not just with the reward but with the fact that a high ranking officer like him could find the time to discuss the sports' interest of a newly recruited constable.

"In early 2004, the IDC championships were held at Nagpur on the Rural Police Grounds. I was then in Nagpur for training. The event was inaugurated with much fanfare in the presence of several senior IPS officers. A separate *pandal* had been set up for the officers and I saw Kamte Sir there. It suddenly prompted me to get up from the ground where we were sitting, to go and meet him. However, I realised that this would be against protocol and therefore I sat down again. I think Kamte Sir had noticed this and as soon as the function was over, he started walking towards us. Many of us rushed forward to meet him. He then told me that I should participate in the 800 metre race the following year. He was such an inspiration to all of us, always prodding us to do better and especially excel in sports.

"Upon returning to Sangli after completing my training in April 2004, Kamte Sir asked us to present a parade. But he wasn't too happy with it and said that our training had not been up to the mark. In July 2004, Kamte Sir was posted at Kolhapur when the inter-region athletics event was organised at Pune. But he made it a point to attend it and on spotting me on the track, he shouted, 'That's my Kumbhar. I have recruited him. He is sure to come first.' After I won the race, he came and put his arm around my shoulder. I will never forget that moment.

"In October 2004 the IDC Championships (in which a cup for the winning team has been instituted in Ashok's grandfather's name, N. M. Kamte) were to be held at Kolhapur. I was selected for the 400 mtrs and 4x400 mtrs relay race. We were asked to congregate for an address by three officers, including Kamte Sir, on the first evening. One of the officers announced that our movements would be restricted during the training sessions and that there would be a roll call thrice a day. We were also instructed not to leave our rooms during the night. This made Kamte Sir very angry. 'Is this a jail? Why should there be restrictions? All we require is a gold medal from them—they should be free to do what they want,' he admonished. He even declared a prize of Rs. 10,000 for the winner. It was an unheard of amount during those days for any police sports event. Kamte Sir would then come and watch us train every evening. He asked me, in particular, to shed some weight. I did so and it certainly helped improve my performance.

"What was remarkable was his knowledge of what diet a sportsman should adhere to. Another time when his guidance was of great help was when I was selected on the rugby team and had to go to Mumbai for practice. Kamte Sir was then in Mumbai with the Anti-Corruption Bureau. We used to train at the Ghatkopar ground and during this time I realised that I was not too comfortable with the game and therefore wished to return to Sangli. Kamte Sir came to know about this and immediately asked me to meet him. He then convinced me that my physique was just right for rugby and that I should not get discouraged so soon. In the 2007 International Championships, our team won and that was a great honour for the Indian Police Force.

"Having imbibed so many values from Kamte Sir, along with journalist Bandopant Rajopadhyay and ten others, I have set up the Late Ashok Kamte Memorial Foundation to instil Kamte Sir's qualities of sportsmanship in youngsters and encourage them to pursue sports seriously, either as a hobby or even as a profession. The foundation has been started in the rural area of Khanapur, Atpadi. Our first step has been to start a gym in village Vita of Sangli district. On November 26, his first death anniversary, we are going to hold a wrestling championship."

Ashok's love for sports spurred him to create sporting facilities for his personnel. As SP Kolhapur, he noticed that there was just one football stadium, the Shahu Football Stadium and entry was restricted to few.

Ashok deployed the staff of the Shahu Football Stadium and converted the police ground into a National level football ground. Entry was unrestricted and youngsters could practice football freely. The ground is made to such high specifications that recently the ONGC Second Division Football League matches were held there, in which international football players participated.

■

CHAPTER 16

FAMILY AND FRIENDS

Ashok was born in Dehra Dun, but Delhi was the city of his childhood. Like most toddlers, Ashok was a very difficult child when it came to feeding, and that he would become a foodie when he grew up, surprised his mother the most. When he was a toddler, feeding him was the biggest nightmare she faced. She would put a bucket of water in front of him to play with, while a servant would amuse him by playing the drum. Even after such tactics, his mother remembers that it took a good two hours to feed him every meal. This drama continued until he was two years old.

For most part of his childhood, Ashok was a boarder. Between 7 and 12 years, he studied in Rajkumar College, Rajkot in Gujarat, a residential school, exclusively set up for princely families of Kathiawad way back in 1838 and now a popular boarding school. Here he excelled in sports, winning the The Wynter-Blyth Memorial Junior School Cup in the year 1974-75 and the Mwanza Cup for the Best Junior Cricketer in the year 1976-77.

When he was 14, he joined the Kodaikanal International School in Kodaikanal, Tamilnadu. This school, initially set up for the children of American Missionaries in 1901, is now a premier residential International School of India. Here too Ashok was outstanding in sports. In the 1979 annual sports event, he broke five school records —in the Pentathlon, 70 yards hurdles, 200 m run, 400 m run and shot putt.

A voracious reader of books, all World War II heroes were his favourites, says his dad, Col. Marutirao Kamte (retd.). Field Marshal Erwin Rommel, a highly decorated and the most famous German army officer of World War II, made an indelible mark on Ashok's mind. As a boy Ashok had an impressive collection of Commando comics, a series of British comic books based on stories of World War I and II. "Whenever he was ill or had to be given medicines as a child, he would demand a book to read," says his father. Ashok addressed his dad as 'General,' probably because he is a walking encyclopaedia of war history. In return, his father called Ashok 'Tiger.' Watching war movies together was their passion and they chatted with each other like the best of friends.

Despite the wonderful relationship he shared with both his parents, his sister Sharmila says that Ashok and she had an emotionally tough childhood. Their parents separated when they were young. His father re-married. Ever since, his mother stays alone in Delhi. Sharmila says, "We had just everything we wanted otherwise. That's why Ashok was more than a brother—he felt an added responsibility towards me, from the time I was a little girl."

Even after entering the Police Service Ashok remained the way he was innately, gentle. At home, he dropped the armour of a tough cop. His booming voice rent the air, but amiably so. If Rahul and Arjun pestered him for attention so did his four dogs who hounded him relentlessly. Whenever he was around, the house reverberated with his favourite music. He had a vast collection of Western music CDs. He would be hooked to a particular number, which he replayed innumerable times, till his ears reached saturation point. At the New Year's Eve party at our home, he would be the DJ, having everyone foot-tapping or dancing to a pulsating mix of music.

As a husband, he was concerned, considerate and affectionate. He never forgot to buy a birthday gift or a Valentine's card for me and organise a surprise party. I was amused when once he went in uniform to buy a Valentine's Day card for me. He loved to make everyone feel special—every member of my family received birthday and wedding anniversary cards from him—he maintained a special calendar for that. Keeping in touch with his friends and colleagues through Diwali, Christmas and New Year was natural for him. In these days of emails and sms's when most of us have forgotten the personal touch of a card, Ashok valued this tradition. He was never too busy for these niceties

My mother, who was one of his best friends, adored his qualities. It was as much a tragedy for her as for me when Ashok passed away. He was like a son for her. She gave vent to her feelings by putting them down in writing.

"Ashok's personality was such that he would be popular with all—from the constable to the highest officers. He had immaculate manners. His personality was a rare combination of simplicity, good nature, smartness and style. This made people love him, adore him and look at him with awe."

She remembers a sari that Ashok bought for her when she had come to visit us in Bhandara. She recalls, "He took me to the famous Bhandara Tusser silk workshop and bought me a sari. Whenever I wore that sari, or for that matter whenever I used any of the numerous presents he had given me, he noticed it without fail. And then with that peculiar boyish innocence he would say excitedly, 'Mummy, I gave this to you, right?' The picture postcards he sent me regularly when he was abroad are my priceless possessions. So are his caring letters that he wrote to me, from time to time."

Ashok would celebrate Christmas with his mother in Delhi without fail, and stay with her for three to four days. Rahul, Arjun and I would also go along with him and very often Sharmila would come down from Dubai for this special family get together. Even on holiday in Delhi, Ashok would make his daily morning calls at nine to check on what was going on in his jurisdiction. His mother would tease him about this and gently admonish him reminding him that he was on holiday.

Everyone in my family loved Ashok because he was transparent and straightforward. He was a warm-hearted host and enjoyed having people home. For my sister Revati, her husband Prashant and their two sons, Diwali was invariably celebrated in our home, no matter where we were posted. Along with them, my parents would also come down. Vandana, Hemant and their two daughters would join us later.

Vandana remembers how "during these holidays, Ashok would make sure that Hemant carried his shoes – as it was a rule of the house that they 'had' to exercise in the evenings along with Ashok. Hemant and Prashant joined Ashok religiously but could never match his speed and stamina and then would slowly slip out for something less strenous."

Ashok would enquire about the menu I had planned for every meal and would give suggestions.

He did not believe in putting up a façade to keep up with social norms. Even if we were hosting a party, Ashok would excuse himself after dinner, when it was his regular time for going to bed. Work, next morning, was so important to him that he never compromised on it.

Ashok also had a great sense of humour. There was never a dull moment with him around and the family get-togethers would always be fun-filled. In fact, he loved jokes and had an impressive repertoire of them. He had a manner of narrating them which kept all in splits.

Ashok never had any chavunistic ideas about being a husband. My cousin Manisha still remembers the time when I went to Malaysia, leaving both the children behind with Ashok in Mumbai. Ashok told my cousin that Rahul would have to be hospitalised due to Falciparum Malaria, and he had to be at work. So Manisha stayed with Rahul. She recalls that Ashok did not even once mention that I should have been there. In fact, he took complete charge of the situation in my absence and never once made me feel guilty about being away.

When he was posted alone in Solapur and Mumbai, I made it a point to visit him at every possible opportunity. Each of these visits was a big holiday for us, without any tensions or demands from him. He would plan the menu for us, and would take care of everybody's likes and preferences. He gave me my space.

Ashok was very meticulous and organised with his belongings. Even if a small thing was out out of place, he would notice it. He was very proud of his college colours which served as nostalgic memories of his school and college days and never discarded them.

Ashok was disciplined in his food habits too. You would never catch him eating a *bhel puri* or a *samosa* or just snacking any time of the day. Morning breakfast would comprise toast and fruits. Lunch would be a big bowl of salad, soup and toast. The only time he indulged himself was at dinner time.

He also enjoyed cooking for his family, friends and probationary officers. Everyone had to have a taste of *'Junglee Maas'* (rustic meat), which he cooked himself. The recipe was as simple as sautéing the meat in asafoetida and whole red chillies until it was tenderly cooked. Then he would add salt to taste and serve it piping hot.

Ashok went in depth in whatever he did. When he had a shoulder injury, he had studied it so thoroughly that he knew the medical terminology of every muscle there, much to the amazement of the orthopaedic surgeon. He would work hard towards recovery, spending an hour in the evening doing stretches for that portion. His library contains many books of medicine, besides those on weaponry and armed warfare tactics. He was well versed with the human anatomy and pharmaceutical drugs. He would never end his day without reading a book. Sometimes, he would complain that we distract him from his reading habit by seeking his attention.

For me, Ashok was a dream come true. Now, he will remain a dream.

The following accounts by Ashok's school mates at the Kodaikanal International School reveal that Ashok was just as gentle, warm and friendly even in those days.

Luis Manta

I first met Ashok in Kodai when I was in the 8th grade. He was a year senior to me. Somehow we hit it off instantly, maybe because we had the same interests, enjoyed the same things and were both ultra-competitive. We spent a lot of time playing games such as four square or basketball or would jog around the lake, lift weights and participate in every sports event we could. We became such good friends that we decided to become roommates the following year. That is how we ended up staying together for the next two years. Later, I left Kodai and then went abroad, which made it difficult to stay in touch. One of the stories Ashok liked to tell about us rooming together was that of one of our first night as roommates. Ashok snored like nobody anyone had ever heard before. I had never been exposed to such noise and though I had heard about this habit, I hadn't really known what to expect. Hence, the first time it happened I jumped out of bed and woke Ashok up telling him there was an animal outside our room. He immediately understood what the source of the noise was and laughed at me for being such a fool. He told this story to anyone and everyone who would listen for the next two years.

After our first quarter together we became eligible for dorm study instead of attending the study hall. This implied that we were allowed to study in our rooms in the evenings. However, Ashok and I had a different idea of what room study meant—to us it was the freedom to do as we pleased. We therefore spent the entire second quarter playing table tennis during the study hours. We both became expert table tennis players but after our grades were announced Ashok took the decision to never opt for room study again.

Ashok was highly competitive and he set for himself ambitious goals. As such, he was an inspiration to others. He always pushed me to train harder and to study better. Mid-way through his junior year he came up with this theory that by cramming in the middle of the night he would do better in his exams since his dreams would tell him what he needed to study. He made this a practice and so every night before an exam he would wake up at around 2 am and study for an hour or so. I don't know if his theory really worked but his grades did improve.

When one begins to recall all such incidents, it seems so unbelievable that Ashok is no longer there. He was a great friend—someone whom you could be proud about. I felt that a piece of me died with him on that day.

Yoshiyuki Fujishima
During my years in Kodaikanal International School between 1979 and 1982, I spent a lot of my time with Ashok. Although I was a year junior to him, we spent several hours at the track, running around the lake and lifting weights. I used to often take care of Ashok's Maths homework. My memory extends to travelling to Ooty for track meets with him. He was my sports rival, true friend and my hero.

The Class of '82 has formed the Ashok Kamte Memorial Fund and instituted a trophy in his name for the best outgoing student of the year. The criteria for the trophy include integrity and leadership; commitment and service to others; good humour; industriousness; perseverence and overall excellence (studies and sports); patriotism and dedication to principles.

Douglas Coudinho
Not many may know of Ashok in his old days. He was pretty much the same guy, good looking with a lot more hair, well built, fair and always passionate about sports and his studies.

Weight lifting was his life in those days and never a day passed without him telling us how much he squatted or how much he benched or deadlifted.

What he did he did with passion, he had a zest for everything he did, yet he remained the same right through his professional and personal life, a down to earth humble soul. I have been a guest at his place on numerous occasions and always appreciated the kind hospitality the Kamtes have extended. What is most striking about Ashok was his love for dogs. At any given time one will see at least 4-5 running around and fawning all over him. I remember very vividly, once we were at his place in Pune and we had finished dinner. While waiting for the dishes to be cleared, Ashok yelled in his authoritative voice for some thing to be brought to the table,to which there was no answer. He shouted again but to no avail. This I found strange because he always had a retinue of people to jump to his orders. At this point he turned to me with a boyish look in his eye and said, "Nobody listens to me in my house," and we had a good laugh. That was Ashok for you. A man who the underworld feared, rogue politicians didn't want to cross swords with and an officer who ruled with an iron hand, yet a loving husband, a doting father and a respectful son.

I would like to add the one person who could make Ashok blush was my darling wife who is no more. She had this uncanny knack of making Ashok literally go pink in his cheeks everytime we would meet. Oh Man! I have never seen Ashok get so tongued tied. I guess we are all brought into this world was for a reason but true friends are few and hard to come by.

I, for one, thank God for Joey, my wife, for Ashok, Vinni and all my close friends who, for me are like diamonds whose shine will never fade, you always wish they will be with you forever.

Himanshu Roy, Joint Commissioner of Police (L&O), Mumbai.

My association with Ashok started in our college days, continued through our training days in the IPS and later through the days of our various postings in Maharashtra. In the college days, it began as a casual association and in the training phase it was a warm friendship and by the time we were into the middle management of the IPS, we were brothers.

No two persons could have been so dissimilar – Ashok and I. He was muscular, I was lean then before I decided to put on muscle like him ; he was tough, I was sensitive; he tried to hide his softer side, I always tried to hide my sterner side, I loved Hindustani music, he liked Western rock; I slept early and rose early and he was the opposite. We were like chalk and cheese. We had our similarities— we were sporting, fun loving, accommodative, hated friction and took our days as they came. Yet , it were the differences which made a perfect foil for a warm friendship which was to grow into a warm relation over the years.

In our college days at the St. Xavier's in Mumbai, Ashok was in the Arts and I was in the Science section and we were just on polite 'hello' terms. In those days, he was a shy, lanky and a somewhat reserved person. He was into sports and excelled even then.

Destiny brought us together again at the National Police Academy (NPA) at Hyderabad, the institution that trains the Indian Police Service (IPS) officers. I was delighted that Ashok too made it to the same cadre which I had been allotted – Maharashtra.

In the NPA , normally each probationer is allotted a room to himself, but due to some renovations two were to share a room for some time. Again, it was a pleasant coincidence that Ashok and I were allotted the same room. As luck would have it, much later, at the Maharashtra Police Academy in Nashik where we went for the induction into the Cadre, we again shared a room.

The differences stood out—my day would begin at 5 in the morning with the strains of some *raga* by Bhimsen Joshi or some other artist and his day would end late at night with some 'rock'. There were so many other differences – we enjoyed them; we were both blessed with the quality of a sporting attitude.

Our room was full of Ashok, always. There will be a number track suites and shorts lying around and so were several pairs of sports shoes, dumbbells, weights, grips, football, etc. There were posters of sports stars (Lothar Matthias was his favorite soccer star). Yes, weapons were his other love and he had a number of books on them. Apart from these, he had little else by way of hobbies. No hanging around with people, no gossips, no group parties. He was warm but somewhat lonely and intense.

If any one quality stood out in Ashok it was his

sportsmanship quality . He was a fighter on the field and in life – he gave it all he had. But once it was over, he took the result sportingly. I had always wondered, how a person who was fighting like a lion till the other moment can so very quickly transform into a soft and gentle person, when the event was over.

He was fiercely competitive and yet he hated friction. In the Academy his outdoor skills and feats became legendary even during our training days. The Drill Instructors (DIs) would compare him with some or the other outstanding officer from earlier batches who excelled in outdoor activities and sports. He was outstanding in athletics, swimming and physical fitness. He was crazy about football , a game in which he excelled; and of course, weightlifting was his passion.

Ashok loved his uniform. Even in the Academy days he tended to it personally, even though we had help to make the uniform. He was probably the best turned out probationer then. This was understandable, coming as he was from a family with a tradition of service in uniform. It was also natural that he had a deep respect and love for his father, a retired Army officer. He was proud of him and his family and of the tradition. He wanted to keep it up.

When Ashok got married, it was one of those rare occasions, when one found him nervous. We were in Pune at that time for our attachment with the State Reserve Police Force and I was glad and amused about his condition. He was lucky to get a vivacious, elegant and a mature companion in Vinita, who was a perfect foil for Ashok as he launched into his career and life.

I and my wife Bhavana along with Ashok and Vinita shared a close bond. It was a blessing which was to last a life time but providence thought otherwise. I lost more than a wonderful colleague and a dear friend.

■

CHAPTER 17

A PASSION FOR WEAPONS

Ashok had an inborn passion for weapons. It came from his own natural aptitude and probably fuelled by the atmosphere he grew up in. He belonged to a family with a long tradition in uniform and it was but natural that since childhood weapons were nothing new to him. This passion, probably, was further fuelled when his dream to get into the Indian Police Service (IPS) was fulfilled—weapons are an integral part of the Service.

Whenever a new weapon was acquired by the Police Force, Ashok always yearned to see it, get familiar with it, handle it and master it. He always displayed a child like wonder when he spoke of, read about or handled new acquisitions. He had a huge collection of books on weapons and tactics and had a couple of favourite book shops in Mumbai and Delhi, which he frequented often looking for the latest books on weapons. When I wondered about his quest for knowledge on weapons and fascination for owning weapons; he would say, it is the requirement of our times.

Even as a child Ashok preferred toy guns over other toys. My mother-in-law often recounts an amusing incident when the family was on a visit to Spain when Ashok was three years old. At a shop, he took fancy to a toy gun too big for him and the parents refused it. Outside, Ashok threw such a tantrum that it attracted attention from passers-by who thought that the parents were not able to afford the toy, so much so that some of them started stuffing coins in Ashok's pockets. The embarrassed parents had no other choice than to go and buy the toy for Ashok.

Ashok's penchant for shooting began when, as a six year old boy, his father gifted him an air gun. At that time, Ashok's family resided in Delhi, in the vicinity of a temple. Excited with his newly acquired gift, Ashok ran to the temple, where he used to spend his leisure hours .Once the priest was seated inside conducting his routine rituals. Ashok aimed at him from the porch of the temple and the pellet struck his back. It was a harmless rubber pellet. Still the startled priest sprang up in fright and turned around to see what hit him. Naturally there was commotion and soon the devotees and the priest identified the 'source' of the pellet. Ashok, stunned at this unexpected turn of events, scampered back home. Within half an hour or so, his mother saw a group of people, angrily entering the house. They were the trustees and some devotees of the temple, coming to protest against Ashok's misconduct. His mother, who was equally aghast, offered them an unconditional apology on behalf of her son. When she reprimanded Ashok for the commotion he had caused, he said he was experimenting with his new air rifle and never realised it would antagonise the priest.

When he became a teenager, Ashok loved to accompany his grandfather for hunting in the outskirts of Delhi, which was not as developed then, and still had thickly wooded areas. They would go hunting during weekends and shoot wild boars and other small animals. Those days hunting used to be legal. Ashok was a shy boy says his mother, and hardly interacted when taken out for parties and social gatherings. However, when he was asked about what he was doing, he would give a reply in mono-syllables, "I shot a boar," and his eyes would twinkle and his lips would break into a smile, says his mother.

Many of his colleagues would visit our home to learn about weapons and he enjoyed enlightening anyone who aspired for knowledge in the subject. I used to be overawed by his passion for weapons and enjoyed every moment of the Sunday when he would ask the children and me to play Bull's Eye with him at home. We always admired his perfect aim.

As a trainee officer at the Maharashtra Police Academy, Nasik, the then Director, Mr. Rahul Gopal and Ashok developed a relationship, rarely shared on par between a greenhorn trainee and a well-established Police Officer. It was the common passion of weapons they shared that brought them close to each other.

Mr. Rahul Gopal had inherited his passion for weapons

from his father, who was an IPS officer of the UP cadre
and an expert at weapons. When Ashok joined the
academy, Mr. Gopal was pleasantly surprised at the
youngster's interest and knowledge of weapons and a
close relationship based on a shared passion ensued. Mr.
Gopal remembers, "Ashok would literally itch to practice
firing. We had a huge firing range at Igatpuri and I offered
Ashok my jeep on the weekends to practice firing there.
He was delighted. At times, I used to also accompany
him."

During this tenure Mr. Rahul Gopal saw and appreciated Ashok's courage and adroitness in handling
weapons against the Naxalites. Mr. Gopal treated Ashok
like a son and was happy to gift him a .45 mm pistol
which Ashok treasured as a part of his collection.

After his stint in Kolhapur, he opted for a posting where
he could train the police force in weaponry and physical
fitness. At the same time, he wanted to have ample time to
spend with the kids and me. Most IPS officers are not keen
on being posted to the Special Security Training Centre in
Pune where policemen and officers are trained to protect
VIPs. Most consider this as an insignificant posting. Ashok
on the contrary was excited when he was posted as the
DIG of this training unit in 2005. He was very satisfied that
he would be handling weapons on a daily basis and would
train officers on men on the subject he loved most—weapon
training and firing. He thoroughly enjoyed his one year tenure
here, when he would personally participate in field training
by experts. Officers and men would be overawed at his felicity
and accuracy with weapons and the enthusiasm with which

he participated despite being the Head of the Institution.

A week before 26/11, the Mumbai Police Commissioner had given him the additional responsibility of co-ordinating with weapon experts from Hong Kong to train the Mumbai Police in the use of sophisticated weapons. He had enjoyed every bit of that assignment.

Prof. Dr. Deepak Rao, Guest Trainer at the Special Security Training Centre in Pune, where Ashok was DIG in 2005, recalls his close association with Ashok:

I am a professional with expertise in Close Quarter Battle, engaged by Indian Forces and Police for various training programs. I was sent to Special Security Training Center in Pune in 2005 where DIG Kamte was the Commandant. That is where I got introduced to him.

Our first meeting was an official one to discuss training for the security officers of the Chief Minister. I remember DIG Kamte as a very fair complexioned, handsome, clean shaven, bald headed by choice. He was muscular and very well built. He was very happy to discuss training and seemed passionate about it.

DIG Kamte would come to the firing range every day during our training sessions. He would personally participate, especially in the firing sessions. He would train side by side with the officers, standing long hours in the scorching sun and shooting round after round.

He fired all the weapons, AK-47s, Sterling Carbines and Glock and Beretta Pistols, emptying magazine after magazine, until all his rounds scored bull's eye.

I admired his acumen. He always had his personal

weapons (pistols and revolvers) which he would keep with him loaded at all times. He would take every opportunity to shoot and target practice to polish his skills. He would make his Officers shoot along with him and then compare the scores of shooting accuracy. The Officers would be embarrassed at their own shooting compared to his perfect shots.

DIG Kamte was into body building and Gymnasium. He had some knee or back problems, for which he sought my advice. He discussed his weight training schedules with me quite a few times. He had a daily schedule which he carried out with clockwork precision. He had perfect discipline and was fully committed to living his personal life—his training, his hobbies and his reading along with his duties as a Police Officer.

A couple of years back, when he was Commissioner of Police, Solapur, he wanted me to make and train a Quick Response Team for Counter Terror Operations. We planned the training enthusiastically, but at the last minute some communal riots broke out due to which the training had to be postponed.

DIG Kamte was a brave officer. He was capable, confident and well trained for that purpose. But providence had other designs. Keeping up with his image, he managed to shoot at the terrorist before he succumbed. Hats off to his bravery! India has certainly lost the most valuable and skilful police officer, who was equipped for the present day terror tactics."

CHAPTER 18

LETTER FROM A FRIEND

One of Ashok's best friends, Conrad Leao, penned this touching letter to Rahul and Arjun after Ashok passed away.

Dear Rahul and Arjun,

Since you probably do not remember meeting me, you will have to take my word for it. Rahul, my strongest memory of you is from a birthday party for my daughter Michelle. You were probably four years old then. One of the boys, who was a year older, was picking on Michelle and you put up your fists in her defense. As they say in this part of the world, 'the apple does not fall far from the tree.' Your father was one of my oldest friends and the only one I stayed in touch with regularly. I am writing to share some of my memories of him. As you grow through the stages of life that he went through, it would be good to remember that the hero was also a boy who became a man.

I met Ashok in 1982 at St. Xavier's College. I had been there for two years when he joined. I remember his faded jeans, tennis shoes and T-shirt, which was almost a uniform for him. We shared most of our classes and got to know each other pretty quickly. You must remember that as boys we were a minority in the Arts classes. It was also the year that the first 'Rambo' movie was released. Bruce Springsteen hit the top of the charts with 'Born in the USA'. It was just a few years after the Soviets had marched into Afghanistan and the deposition of the Shah of Iran. We did not know then that some of these events would in turn influence our lives so tragically.

Ashok was very different from me with his athletic abilities. But we shared a common interest in the military — me in military history and him in military practice. He encouraged me to train with weights and made sure my technique and form was correct. Every time I do squats or bench-press I cannot forget his instructions, even now. At that time 'Eye of the Tiger' from the 'Rocky' movie series was one of his favourite songs that helped pump him up. He was unique in his ability to commit himself entirely to his ambitions. He simply had to be the best at whatever he did. His athletic success in diverse sports from soccer to powerlifting seemed to be driven by his belief that an athlete should be able to succeed in any sport - though he did somewhat ruefully speak of his struggles in the pole vault when he competed in the decathlon.

If I remember right, he wore the number 10 when he played Centre Forward at Xavier's on the soccer team.

He was quite proud of how the spectators would applaud the performance of *"dus number"*. Of course any remembrance of your father cannot omit food. He loved food. He had a tremendous appetite and was very particular about getting all the nourishment he needed to support his intense workouts. I remember hanging out in his hostel room after a workout while he mixed his milkshake with a few raw eggs and maybe a protein supplement thrown in.

He was the only person I have ever known who had a budget for milk. We would go sometimes to the dairies around our college and have a saucer of fresh cream with some sugar sprinkled over it, or a thick *lassi* with a dollop of cream on top. What he never failed to remind me every time we met since college was how we concluded each exam with a meal at my house. I think my mother was half terrified and half pleased when he came over - terrified that she had not made enough and pleased because he enjoyed her cooking so much.

We were a trio of friends—your Dad, Vinod Chacko and myself. We were as unlikely a combination as Laurel and Hardy - your dad with his powerful frame, Vinod who was as thin as anyone could possibly be but with an unexpectedly deep voice, and myself. After college we lost touch with Vinod for a long while. When I met your father last June we talked about it and he asked if I could track Vinod down through the Internet. I took it on for his sake and was able to find Vinod soon after I returned to the US.

The thing that I like to remember most about Ashok

in college is that in spite of his tremendous success on the sports field he never dropped the ball on his studies. I am sure that it must have been tempting, given his long days and many hours of training. Yet he made sure that he worked at his books as hard as he could and turned in a performance that most other students would have been proud of. He never showed up late for class though he had been given the slack to do so. Of course he had my phone number memorised, so that he could check if he was studying for the right exam. He was the first to laugh about the times he got his exam dates scrambled.

At that time we were all unclear as to what we would do after we graduated. Except for Ashok. He was always clear that he would opt for the army or the police. Could he have been a sports star in today's world? I am sure he could. However, from what I know of him that would not have been a choice he would have made. Did you know that your Dad could ride a scooter? I visited him at his home in Delhi after college, when my company sent me to Delhi for training. After dinner he dropped me back to the company guest house on his scooter. I forget the model but I think it may have been a Vijay. He was studying for the civil service exams at that point. And he still had all his hair!

A funny thing about knowing him for so long is that between the times he used to come to my house in an autorickshaw to the time he came to my house in a staff car with an escort, his fundamental personality did not alter. The boy did not leave the man. He still laughed as heartily. Something else that always struck me as unique about him was his warmth. Personally I am not a very demonstrative person, but Ashok would always be the first to give me a hug when we met or were saying goodbye. I hope you have inherited that trait from him.

In 1991 I asked him to be the 'best man' at my wedding. Against all odds he made it to Mumbai to stand at my side as I got married. He is part of the wedding picture on my parents' mantelpiece in Mumbai since then and on my picture-stand here in my home at New Jersey. I am sure his job had tough moments, many of them. When he first started as an ASP, before he was married, he would call up to chat after such moments. Since I moved to the US in 1998 our meetings were few. The last time we met was in June and July of 2008. We had dinner in June at my place. We ate and drank perhaps more than we should have for a couple of middle-age guys. He was proud of what he had accomplished so far in the IPS. He hoped to be the Commissioner of Police at Mumbai some day. To me that was his modesty speaking. We both knew that it would just be a milestone along the way.

We joked about why he would never take up a job in Europe, America, Australia or Canada. That's because he was too fond of his life in India with all the household help readily available. But mostly we talked about how proud he was of both of you. A little nervous, maybe, that Rahul did not like studying as much as sports, but immensely proud. For someone who was so comfortable walking a solitary path the respect that he expressed for what your mom thought of him and the love he had for his boys was a pleasure to see. The memory of these moments is something I cherish because at these times we were just two guys talking about our lives The DIG and the VP personalities were shelved for the evening.

When I visited him at his office in Chembur a few weeks later, he took me to see his rented house. He pointed out the features that he thought would make it a great place for you to stay. It was a really nice place and he was looking forward to the three of you enjoying it. In the last few months, I have seen so much written about him. It is apparent that he made friends and earned respect through his lifetime. I believe that he died a death characterised by courage and a sense of personal responsibility toward his role that goes beyond any man's responsibility to a job. But the important thing to remember is that his actions that night were no surprise to those who knew him.

His actions were the natural reaction of who he was, not just what (a police officer) he was. For me his courage was not in his being a police officer but rather in how he lived as one. All the training, skills and abilities in the world cannot give a man courage over and above the call of duty. That is the example he has set for those of us who stay behind in this world. To choose the 'who' we want to be. The 'what' will follow. As you grow up the sense of loss may never go away, but you have the opportunity to be the men he would have wanted you to be. Be happy when you do that, because he is looking at you from another world, and he will be proud and happy.

— *Conrad Leao*

CHAPTER 19

A New Day, A New Dream

R ahul always nurtured a dream of studying at the
Kodaikanal International School, inspired as he was
by the stories Ashok narrated to him. The star attraction
being sports treated on par with academics. Rahul too,
an avid sportsperson like Ashok, plays tennis, table tennis,
cricket and volleyball extensively. However, it was after
Ashok passed away that he insisted on seeking admission
there, this year itself.

"Complete your present academic session of Std X
here in Pune and then pursue your Std XI and Std XII
there," I advised him when he broached the topic early
this year. He stood firm though. I did not want to argue
too much as perhaps the void of Ashok's loss was too
hard to fill. Perhaps, he needed a break from my constant
talk in the house revolving around Ashok and my
investigations.

The school authorities, in fact, had got in touch with
me after Ashok's demise and had offered to educate both

the children, whom they considered as part of their social responsibility. I was deeply moved by this gesture.

Sharmila too had been a boarder in that school and often told me how Ashok, seven years her elder, played the father figure to her. She said she would to be overawed by him, in fact a bit shy. Being handsome and an outstanding student, heads would turn when Ashok walked around the school campus. I discussed with her about Rahul's desire to take admission there, as she had come down to Pune for a short break, from Dubai, early this year.

Sharmila thought it was a good idea. She said, "The environment is so charming – it is the right place for Rahul to break away from the emotional ordeal and pursue his love for sports." In an instant though, tears welled up. Most of her memories of her brother are locked inside the sylvan surroundings of this elite school, where Ashok played the ideal role of a doting elder brother.

Her journey up to the hill station, twice a year, would be peppered with the beauty of the charming landscape and the agony of travel sickness. And of how affectionately Ashok would take care of her in her suffering. In fact, from the time they left Delhi, he would ensure that she had her motion sickness tablets. She reminisces, "It used to be in the thick of the monsoon season when our new term started. We literally used to pass through the clouds and colourful flora, as our bus meandered through the 45-kilometre *ghat*. The richness of nature's glory though used to be blurred by the nauseating feeling that overwhelmed me. Even the medication that I carried along with me wouldn't help. It was only Ashok's tender care that saw me through the sickness."

Sharmila said she would rest her head on Ashok's shoulder the moment the bus began its climb. Putting his sturdy arm around her, he hoped each time she would withstand the journey. The drama would always be invariably thus:

"Driver, zara bus roko!" Ashok would shout from his seat, when Sharmila would gesture to him that she wanted to throw up. Pushing himself ahead, with Sharmila's thin arms firmly in his grip, both would alight from the bus. He would then escort her to the roadside. Later, he would take out an orange lozenge from his shirt pocket and tell her to keep it in her mouth. He always made sure he bought a few of these sweets before the journey.

"We were divided because of our age difference," and hence, she recollects, "I used to feel shy of his awesome presence and the stardom he had achieved in school. Girls would adore him not only for his good looks but for his super athlete image. They used to prod me to go and say Hi to him but I would always hide from him. He would then wave out and call me. He would ask me whether I wanted an ice-cream. And even before I replied he would give me money to buy one. Teachers, she says, used to be amazed at his attention and protectiveness towards me."

In fact, Ashok was so protective of Sharmila that on two occasions, he had bashed up eve-teasers, recollects his father. While he was studying for his civil services examination in Delhi, Sharmila went for her dancing lessons in the evenings. The only break Ashok took from his studies was to drop her and fetch her from there. "Even in the chilliest of the Delhi winter," recollects Sharmila, "he would come on a scooter to pick me up."

"He also encouraged my sporting activities and attended the school's sports events. He would always be there to cheer his 'Bugs Bunny' as he fondly called me."

In late July, I set off on the journey to Kodaikanal with Rahul. Vandana too joined me. It was not the first time that Rahul was going as a hostelite. When we were posted to Sangli, he was a boarder at the Sanjeevani School in Panchgani for four years. This time though he was excited as he was going to study in his father's alma mater. I was glad to escort him to a place where he was keen to go.

The undulating Pali hills were lined with stocky trees. Lofty eucalyptus *(Nilgiri)* and other seemingly sky-high trees form a soaring, lush green canopy above you. The fragrance of the eucalyptus fleets by and the chill breeze compels you to close the car window.

Kodaikanal was re-discovered in 1845 by the American missionaries and British bureaucrats to escape the Chennai heat that became oppressive in the hot months. In fact, the Kodaikanal International School was set up for the children of American missionaries in 1901. Today the students hail from 30 different countries and the cross-cultural exchange broadens a student's perspective of life, besides making him into an all-rounder.

We reached Kodaikanal and settled at a resort before making our way to the school. We reached the school, which borders a main road filled with hustle-bustle, but once you enter the gate, you are transported into a rustic English countryside landscape. Two gigantic trees stand slimly like two veteran guards on either side of the entrance, standing mute testimony to every new generation that crosses them. The name of the school is engraved humbly within the framework of an unevenly cut stone. Dotted with manicured lawns, lofty trees and undulating winding paths, a series of single-storied structures in Gothic architecture represent different segments of the school.

The Kodaikanal International School campus over-looks a large man-made lake called Kodi Lake. It has three campuses representing different levels of the school, with several dormitories. Rahul was accommodated in the Penryn dormitory. Quite thoughtfully, Mr. and Mrs. Balachander, who were very fond of Ashok when he was in school, took over Rahul's charge.

We were warmly welcomed by Mrs. Balachander. She remembered Ashok as being a most obedient, focused and affable student. She reminesced, "Ashok was one of the rare students who always remembered to send a Christmas card every year, although he had passed out from school many years back." She showed me his card she had received in the Christmas of 2007.

Mr. B (this is how Mr. Balachander is addressed in school) was Ashok's Physical Education teacher. He presently is the Dean. Ashok was his favourite student. He recalled, "Ashok was much focused even as a teenager. While other boys of his age would think of having fun during leisure hours, Ashok would be found in the gym at 6 pm sharp. Always ready to help, Mr. B recalled how Ashok voluntarily accompanied him on a search for one of the boys who had gone missing in the nearby hills after a trekking expedition. The boy was found three days later, as he had strayed into the thick forest by mistake.

"Don't worry, we will take good care of Rahul," they assured me. I felt secure, just as Rahul did.

I hoped Rahul would get serious about studies here. Not that it would have bothered Ashok. Whenever I used to be worried, or hauled up the children for studies, he would smile and say, "Let them learn their way and at their own pace. At the most, they may not perform well—that too will be a learning experience for them."

Vandana and I unpacked his belongings in the room he would be sharing with another boy. I was most amused to note that while we were still unpacking, Rahul was already off to play lawn tennis. Within the two days that we were there, Rahul had already familiarised himself with the place and he got busy playing games.

I was quite pleased though when Mr. B told me before leaving, "He seems to have a good hand at lawn tennis, and we will make sure we hone his skills." It revealed the school's enthusiasm to spot talent.

It was time to leave Rahul behind and go back to Pune.
I was relieved that Rahul was well settled in his new
surroundings, However, there was still a feeling of
emptiness at having Rahul away from home.

I came back home to my father-in-law, Arjun and the
four lovable dogs. Rahul, unlike Ashok, got busy in his
own world. That had my mother-in-law in Delhi
reminding me, when I visited her a couple of months
later, "I haven't received a single letter or email from
Rahul." I smiled. She was used to Ashok who always
remembered to be in touch with each and every family
member, on every occasion.

Once, while I was lazing in bed in the afternoon, Arjun
kissed me and said, "I also want to go to Kodaikanal
International School, but then who will look after you?
You will feel lonely?" In an effort to reassure him, I smiled
and told him, "No, why should I feel lonely? I will find
things to do and will be happy to see you both well-
settled in the same school. I can always come and spend
a few weeks with both of you." I know that soon he
would also pursue his dreams in that picturesque
landscape which gave their Dadda the formidable
foundation in life.

The name Ashok itself means 'beyond grief.' All of us
are trying to go beyond grief to find our bearings.

Ashok loved the soulful number *'Tere bin'* sung by
Pakistani artist, Atif Aslam in the album *'Bas Ek Pal,'*
and I wish to end this book with excerpts from its lyrics.
He had recorded this song 20 times on his ipod and would
play it every evening when he was posted in Solapur,

where he lived alone without us. His staff knew about his liking for this number. His constables had recorded it on their mobiles, as he would put forward his *farmaish* of listening to it when his ipod was not with him. This song now has a special significance in my life:

'Tere bin main yun kaise jiya
Kaise jiya tere bin
Tere bin main yun kaise jiya
Kaise jiya tere bin
Lekar yaad teri raaten meri kati - 2
Mujhse baaten teri karti hai chaandani
Tanha hai tujh bin raaten meri
Din mere din ke jaise nahi...'

TRANSLATION: ...

Without You ...
Without you, how did I live like this?
How did I live without you?
Without you, how did I live like this?
How did I live without you?
With your memories, my nights pass
The moonlight talks to me about you
My nights are lonely without you
My days are no longer like days.

■

BIO-DATA: ASHOK KAMTE

Ashok Marutirao Kamte

Date of birth: February 23, 1965, in Dehradun

School education: Rajkumar College, Rajkot
Kodaikanal International
School, Kodaikanal

College education: St. Xavier's College, Mumbai
(B A in History and English)
St.Stephen's College, Delhi
(M A in History)
Defence Services Staff College,
Wellington, Tamilnadu
(M Sc Defence & Strategic
Studies)
Selected to Indian Police
Services - 1989 batch

Postings:

Assistant Superintendent of
Police, Bhandara:
November 1991-January 1994
Superintendent of Police,
Satara:
January 1994 to May 1996
Defence Services Staff College,
Wellington:
June 1996-April 1997
Superintendent of Police,Thana:
May 1997- June 1999
UN peace keeping mission in
Bosnia:
July 1999 -July 2000
Deputy Commissioner, Zone I,
Mumbai:
August 2000 to August 2002
Superintendent of Police,
Sangli:
August 2002- July 2004
Superintendent of Police,
Kolhapur:
August 2004- March 2005
Additional Commissioner of
Police, Anti-Corruption Bureau
March 2005-May 2005
Deputy Inspector General
(DIG), Special Security Training
Centre:
June 2005-July 2006

Police Commissioner, Solapur:
August 2006 to June 2008
Additional Commissioner, East
Mumbai Region:
June 2008 until he passed away
on November 26, 2008

Medals: Special Service Medal, Naxalite
Operations: 1995
UN Medal for service in Bosnia:
1999-2000
Videsh Seva Medal for service
in Bosnia: 2000
DG's Signia for Outstanding
Service: 2004
Antarik Suraksha Padak for
Anti-Naxalite Operations: 2005
Police Medal for meritorious
service: 2006

Sports: Father Fell Silver Jubilee Trophy
of St Xavier's College, Mumbai
for the best all rounder
sportsperson: 1983-84
Maharashtra Amateur Athletic
Association, first place in Shot
Putt (under 19 years): 1st place:
1983-84
Maharashtra Power Lifting
Association, Nagpur,

1st place in 100kg weight class.
(Total weight lift: 640 kgs.
Full Squat: 235 kgs; Back Press:
160kgs; Dead Lift: 245 kgs)
10th Delhi State Power Lifting
Championship,
1st place in 100kgs weight class:
1987
National Power Lifting
Championship,
1st place in 100 kgs weight class:
January 1987
National Police Academy,
Hyderabad, 1991:
Trophy for unarmed combat;
Maharaja Singh Cup for games
and sports; R D Singh cup for
swimming, and Senior Officers'
Trophy for best turnout.

Ashok Kamte was the recipient of India's
highest peacetime gallantry award, the Ashok
Chakra, posthumously in 2008 for his valour in
combatting the terrorists on 26/11/2008 during
the attack in Mumbai.

■

Doting Mother Pramila
with Baby Ashok

Sharmila with big
brother Ashok

Little Ashok all set to be a cop

Teenager Ashok–
a super athlete

Winner of the Father Fell Trophy
at St. Xavier's College in the year
1983-84 for the best sportsperson

Ashok showcases his
shotputting skills at the
Police Games in Sangli

From left: Chhatrapati Shahu Maharaj,Ashok,
Chhatrapati Sambhaji Raje and Chhatrapati
Maloji Raje at a football exhibition match in
Kolhapur, in memory of National level
football player, Mahadev Gharge

Ashok with his mother Pramila and sons, Rahul and Arjun

Ashok and his sister Sharmila relaxing in Dubai

Vinita and Ashok at their home

Happy times with friends in Solapur: (from left): Sunil, Yatin, Col Sanjay and Ashok

The family album: Vinita and Ashok with Vinita's parents, sisters and their families

Celebrating Col.Kamte's 75th Birthday - Col. Kamte,his wife Kalpana and the Kamte Family

Toddler Rahul with Ashok relaxing at their Satara home

Ashok with his favourite pet, Hazel in Sangli

Ashok (right) with Arjun and father, Col Marutrao Kamte

Ashok, leading a police team to fight Naxalites in the hostile terrain of Bhandara, where he was posted as Assistant Superintendent of Police (ASP)

Ashok, as a young ASP with Mr Francis Aranha (centre) his then boss, Superintendent of Police

Ashok in full action, quelling riots outside Mantralaya after the Vilasrao Deshmukh Government won the vote of confidence in 2002

Ashok in action, controlling riots in Solapur

Ashok with his DCPs,
Mr. Budhwant and
Mr. Warke at a major road
junction in Solapur during
curfew time

In Bosnia, during an
assignment for the
UN Peace Keeping Mission

I believe in 'Shastra
puja' (weapon worship):
Ashok

Testing the quality of a
bullet-proof jacket in Mumbai

Great grandfather Marutirao Kamte

Ashok's grandfather Narayanrao M Kamte, first Inspector General of Bombay State of Independent India with Pandit Jawaharlal Nehru during the latter's visit at the Police Mess in Nashik

Ashok's father Col Marutirao Kamte with the then President of India, Dr Sarvapalli Radhakrishnan

Ashok as Additional Commissioner, East Region,
quelling riots at Deonar, Chembur, in mid-2008